ALL IN THE SAME BOAT

Also by Warren FitzGerald

Fiction:
The Go-Away Bird

www.warrenfitzgerald.co.uk

ALL IN THE SAME BOAT

THE UNTOLD STORY OF THE BRITISH FERRY CREW
WHO HELPED WIN THE FALKLANDS WAR

WARREN FITZGERALD

Sam

Best Wishes,

[signature]

JB

JOHN BLAKE

First published by
John Blake Publishing Limited
3 Bramber Court, 2 Bramber Road
London W14 9PB

www.johnblakebooks.com

www.facebook.com/johnblakebooks 🇫
twitter.com/jblakebooks 🇪

First published in hardback in 2016

ISBN: 978-1-78606-006-8

British Library Cataloguing-in-Publication Data:

A catalogue record for this book is available from the British Library.

Design by www.envydesign.co.uk

Printed in Great Britain by CPI Group (UK) Ltd

1 3 5 7 9 10 8 6 4 2

Papers used by John Blake Publishing are natural, recyclable products made
from wood grown in sustainable forests. The manufacturing processes
conform to the environmental regulations of the country of origin.

Every attempt has been made to contact the relevant copyright-holders,
but some were unobtainable. We would be grateful if the
appropriate people could contact us.

To all the unsung heroes. In peacetime and war.

CONTENTS

PROLOGUE: 1982   1

1: RUM, BUM AND BACCY   19

2: WHO'S THE POOF ON THE PIANO?   45

3: A SLIGHT CHANGE OF PLAN   71

4: FROM TEA AND BUNS TO   83
   SUBMACHINE GUNS

5: SHHH!   95

6: LCU, NGS, Y2K AND G&T   103

7: READ ALL ABOUT IT! MERCHANT SHIP   115
   SUNK IN FALKLANDS

8: THE PRISON SHIP   133

9: TRENCH FOOT AND TENDERNESS   147

10: FROM SEA KINGS AT DAWN TO   173
    MOWING THE LAWN

11: COLLAPSING UNDER THE STRAIN   191

12: THE GRAND FINALE?   207

13: I WOULD HAVE MUCH PREFERRED A   215
NICE BROOCH

14: THE LOVE BOAT   221

15: GATHERING DUST AND RISING   233
TENSIONS

EPILOGUE   241

ACKNOWLEDGEMENTS   249

APPENDIX I: CREW LIST – MV *NORLAND*   251
AS OF 11 MAY 1982

APPENDIX II: OFFICERS' DUTIES   259

APPENDIX III: TECHNICAL DATA   261

FURTHER READING   263

PROLOGUE
1982

In the spring of 1982 Prince Charles and Princess Diana had (apparently) been happily married for nearly a year. Their first baby, oblivious of the tribulations that lay ahead for him, was on the way, developing securely in its mother's womb. By contrast, in the bottom of a test tube in a laboratory in Cambridge, other babies were being conceived in revolutionary IVF experimentation. If you were learning about this news from your TV at home, there would have been only three channels to choose from. But if you'd rather play *Hungry Horace* or *Breakout* you'd be playing on your Commodore 64 or ZX Spectrum, the cutting edge of gaming technology.

Spielberg's latest film *E. T.* was out in cinemas although some of us were too busy marvelling at our new Betamax or VHS video players, which enabled us to watch movies at home whenever we chose to, as long as we schlepped down to the video shop first to hire them. *Rocky III* was also playing and a song from the movie, *Eye of The Tiger* by American rock band Survivor was all over the radio, competing with British groups such as Duran Duran, Human League, Bananarama, Soft Cell and the soon to be defunct The Jam. In the pop bands and in the streets there was a lot of mousse, hairspray and highlights making big hair; and in the playground the fashionable boys were wearing sta press trousers, a waffle cardigan, white socks and grey slip-on shoes. After school the white socks would be swapped for luminous orange or day-glo green, the trousers would be white (or burgundy for special occasions) and the cardigan pastel coloured courtesy of Fosters or Burtons. The girls would be in pleated skirts or pleated trousers with leg warmers in the style of the kids from *Fame*.

The grown-ups (the men at least) were sporting moustaches à la Tom Selleck in the hit TV show *Magnum PI*, very short shorts in the good weather and leather jackets à la Bodie from *The Professionals* when it was chilly. The ladies were in dungarees, inspired by Dexy's Midnight Runners who were climbing the charts with *Come On Eileen,* and they were shopping in the newest women's clothing store to hit the high street: Next.

According to Michael Jackson and Paul McCartney, ebony and ivory were living in perfect harmony, but in Maggie Thatcher's Britain things weren't so harmonious. In January unemployment had hit three million for the first time since 1930, her son Mark had gone missing in the Sahara while taking part in the Dakar Rally and the miners were contemplating strike action. They actually voted against it and accepted a 9.3 per cent pay rise. It would be another couple of years before their mammoth year-long strike as they went head to head with Maggie in a war over pit closures that would bring many mining communities to their knees.

In March of 1982 Mary Whitehouse was also waging war against the National Theatre for indecency in the play *The Romans in Britain*, while on the other side of the planet a party of Argentine scrap-metal dealers sailed into Leith harbour in the remote and inhospitable island of South Georgia six hundred miles east of the Falkland Islands. They were part of a company apparently contracted to dismantle an abandoned whaling station on the British-owned island, the only inhabitants of which were a handful of Brits constituting an Antarctic Survey Team. But Argentine marines had infiltrated the scrap-metal dealers' ship as a means of establishing a base of their own on the disputed territory, so when the ship docked they went ashore and raised an Argentinian flag. There were no scrap-metal dealers – they were all marines in civvies.

The Brits politely (of course!) asked the uninvited guests to take down the flag and leave. The marines refused, so Maggie, ever up for a fight at home or abroad, had no hesitation in sending twenty-two Royal Marines straight over to the island on board HMS *Endurance*, an ice patrol ship, which was in the vicinity of the Falklands at the time.

While government eyes were focused on *Endurance* chasing the scrap-metal dealers' ship around South Georgia, on 2 April Argentine forces invaded the Falkland Islands, another territory they had disputed ownership of since 1833; islands which every textbook in Argentina calls *Las Islas Malvinas*. The following day, a relatively small group of Argentine marines took South Georgia. The invasion of the Falklands, however, was a far bigger affair. Argentina was sending in thousands of troops, so Maggie sent thousands of British ones to turf them out of the barren, windswept islands, a few hundred miles off the Argentinian coast, which nearly two thousand Brits called home.

I was nine years old at the time and so the news on TV was

something to be endured on a Thursday in order to get to *Top of the Pops* afterwards, when I could revel in performances of my favourite bands of the moment, Wham and Culture Club among them. So on Thursday, 1 April, when the newscasters talked about tensions in the South Atlantic on some rock thousands of miles away, I wasn't really interested. I was even less interested a few days later in hearing the Prime Minister's soporifically posh voice coming from the TV saying:

> Mr Speaker, sir, the House meets this Saturday to respond to a situation of great gravity. We are here because for the first time in many years British sovereign territory has been invaded by a foreign power. After several days of rising tension in our relations with Argentina, that country's armed forces attacked the Falkland Islands yesterday and established military control…The government has now decided that a large task force will sail as soon as all preparations are complete. HMS *Invincible* will be in the lead and will leave port on Monday.

★   ★   ★

At the Court at Windsor Castle
THE 4th DAY OF APRIL 1982
PRESENT,
THE QUEEN'S MOST EXCELLENT
MAJESTY IN COUNCIL

Whereas it is expedient in view of the situation now existing in relation to the Falkland Islands that Her Majesty should be enabled to exercise in the most effectual manner the powers at law vested in Her for the defence of the realm including Her Majesty's dependent territories: —

Now, therefore, her Majesty is pleased, by and with the advice of her Privy Council, to order, and it is hereby ordered, as follows:

1. This Order may be cited as the Requisitioning of Ships Order 1982.

2. A Secretary of State or the Minister of Transport (hereinafter referred to as 'the Minister') or the Lords Commissioners of the Admiralty may requisition for Her Majesty's service any British ship and anything on board such ship wherever the ship may be.

3. A Secretary of State or the Minister of Transport or the Lords Commissioners of the Admiralty may, to such extent and subject to such conditions and restrictions as he or they think proper, delegate all or any of his or their functions under Article 2 of this Order to any specified persons or class of persons.

4. The owner of any ship or thing requisitioned under this Order shall receive such payment for the use thereof during its employment in Her Majesty's service and such compensation for loss or damage to the ship or thing occasioned by such employment as may be provided by any enactment related to payment or compensation in respect of the exercise of powers conferred by this Order and, in the absence of such an enactment, such payment or compensation as may be agreed between a Secretary of State or the Minister of Transport or the Lords Commissioners of the Admiralty (as the case

may be) and the owner or, failing such agreement, as may be determined by arbitration.

5. In this Order:—

'Secretary of State' means any of Her Majesty's Secretaries of State;

'Requisition' in relation to any ship or thing means take possession of the ship or thing or require the ship or thing to be placed at the disposal of the requisitioning authority;

'British Ship' means a ship registered in the United Kingdom or any of the following countries:—

(a) the Isle of Man;

(b) any of the Channel Islands;

(c) any colony;

(d) any country outside Her Majesty's dominions in which her Majesty has jurisdiction in right of the government of the United Kingdom.

N. E. Leigh,

Clerk of the Privy Council

And so the Falklands War ensued. For me and everyone I knew, not having relatives in the armed forces who fought in that war, I was relatively untouched by the events. In the subsequent years I was disturbed by images and reports from the conflict, as I was any war overseas, I was horrified by the story of Simon Weston, probably the most famous veteran of the Falklands, and struggled to look at his scarred face as much as I struggled to understand what or who could have done that to him. But this is the lot of a soldier, is it not? War is horrific and when you join the armed forces you are signing up for a part in a possible war.

PROLOGUE

It was over thirty years later, and *Top of the Pops* unfortunately a thing of the past, when I was watching the BBC's latest magazine programme, having just sat through the news with much more interest than my nine-year-old self, but with far more irritation at the depressing catalogue of negativity it constituted. However, the gloom was about to be lifted by the vision of a white-haired man in a pink satin shirt playing piano and getting everyone in the studio in the mood for a good old fashioned knees up. He told the story of his experience in the Falklands conflict all those years ago, as a steward on board a passenger ferry transporting troops from Portsmouth to the battle zone. This very camp figure told the presenters, with his engaging East Yorkshire turn of phrase, how he had won over the generally homophobic troops both with his piano playing and his efforts to look after the soldiers on their way to this brief but brutal war and I, always on the look out for inspiration for my next work of fiction, made a note in my phone that this sounded like the good premise for a novel.

The vision of this gay steward, Roy 'Wendy' Gibson, stayed with me, not least because his story illuminated my own ignorance about the fact that passenger ferries and their crews, as well as other ships in the Merchant Navy, could be and are often requisitioned by the government to support Royal Navy battleships in times of war, as the hastily drawn up Order in Council quoted above shows all too clearly. And, as Roy was to tell me himself in characteristically modest style, when I was honoured to meet him a few months later, 'It wasn't just Wendy's war.' There were ninety-nine crew members on his ship, the *Norland*, alone, who were also roped into that war and a number of them, like Roy, were gay.

In fact, a significant proportion of all merchant seamen, usually among the catering or hospitality staff, were gay. For example on the *Canberra*, a luxury cruise liner, much bigger than the *Norland*, which could carry two thousand passengers and had a crew of around a thousand, nearly half of the crew, according to one of the stewards on its maiden voyage in the 1960s, were homosexual. Nearly all merchant seamen before the mid-1980s were men. Women were pretty much excluded from the profession, as they were from many others. And perhaps this in itself is reason enough to explain why so many men on the merchant ships were gay. Out on the high seas for days, weeks or even months on end trapped on a boat with nothing but men for colleagues and company, must have been very appealing for a gay man, especially when on land being gay was something society still told them to be ashamed of. Homosexuality was only decriminalized in 1967 and was still illegal in the armed forces, incredibly, until 1999. On land, getting spat at or even beaten up in the streets for being gay was commonplace and, caught between that rock and the hard place of being arrested, no wonder many men fled to the high seas, away from the draconian jurisdictions and the threat of violence.

However, as with the armed forces, homosexuality was also technically illegal in the Merchant Navy until 1999, and why should the threat of violence or intimidation to a gay man be any less on a boat out on the ocean with a load of straight men aboard? Well, as Roy and other crew members of the *Norland*, gay and straight, were to inform me, there were a number of reasons. I get the sense that the main reason was a culture of 'live and let live' which seemed to permeate the Merchant Navy ships. By signing up to a life at sea, all crew members were eschewing normal life to a certain extent. Travel broadens the mind, they say, and this certainly seems to be the case with the crew members I have met during the course of writing this book. Out on the ocean the safety of the passengers and the smooth running of the ship were paramount and so the crew tended to pull together in a unique way, with no room for petty squabbles and irreconcilable differences. Grafters were welcome on board. You did not tend to be judged by your sexuality on the merchant ships, but more so by how hard you worked, and this judgement came from both the gay and straight crew members.

Besides, some of the heterosexual men, having been away from their wives or girlfriends for weeks or months on end, would sometimes 'love the one they're with' themselves, in a 'what goes on on tour stays on tour' kind of way. Other closeted homosexuals found this world away from home the perfect place to exercise their real sexual desires in a way they never dared to on land. And the openly gay men in the crew were often happy to help them out.

Many, but not all, of these openly gay men were incredibly and wonderfully camp. As a Brit, I think camp needs no explanation, but since just the other day a friend from North America asked me to explain what the word meant, I will do so here. Camp is the stuff of the mainstream comedy we grew up with in 1970s England. Seaside postcard humour, Larry Grayson, Frankie Howerd, John Inman in *Are You Being Served?* Kenneth Williams in the *Carry On* films. And if we think we've 'risen above' all that now think again of the most popular comedy shows and performers of recent years: Julian Clary, Paul O'Grady, David Walliams in *Little Britain,* or, for my North American buddy, RuPaul.

With the advent of the Gay Liberation movement in the late

1970s and early 1980s there was a pressure to find camp outmoded and pandering to negative stereotypes concerning gay men. But camp is about theatricality, effeminacy, 'cheese' and kitsch, not just about being gay or dressing up in drag, and so it still has a great role to play in breaking down barriers between the sexes and exploring through comedy more facets of being human than gender stereotypes would traditionally permit.

The camp men who flounced up the gangways eager to embark on the next job with the Merchant Navy were not being camp for laughs, they were not performing to millions of families sitting at home on a Saturday night watching Larry Grayson on the telly. They were just being themselves. And finally, on the Merchant Navy ships, they had found somewhere they could do this without fear. In fact on some ships they were the majority. The rest were outnumbered. And, unfortunately for some, there is always safety in numbers.

Despite the archaic laws, the shipping companies such as North Sea Ferries (which was to become P&O in the 1990s) actually encouraged camp gay men to take jobs on their ships in the catering (or hospitality) departments (the crew usually being divided into catering, navigation and engineering). Men like Roy 'Wendy' Gibson. Why? Well, for the North Sea Ferry officers, they knew that the 'feminine' touch, those little extra flourishes which the passengers loved – attention to detail in the presentation of their cabins, the fuss made over them at dinner, the immaculate appearance of the steward himself – was never going to be provided by the straight scruffy bloke reluctantly doing a short-term contract on the ships while there wasn't much work for him on the buses in Hull.

So, as Roy described it himself, there was a harmonious

'floating village' on the *Norland* in 1982. As with gangs of lads all over the world, nicknames, rituals, and initiations were de rigeur on the ship, but unlike many other gangs of lads, heterosexuality was not. And when the crew of the *Norland* had to swap the ladies in their evening gowns and European holiday makers for a thousand paratroopers, known for their ferocity at work and at play, the tinderbox was set.

Hence it wasn't just Wendy's war. It wasn't even every gay man's war on that ship. It was every single crew member who found their little world away from normality floating into another world even further removed from the everyday, but in all the wrong ways. All this, however, I was still to discover as I managed to track down Roy via another crew member in Hull, Keith Thompson.

Keith was the assistant purser on the *Norland* in 1982. Now, I might have been up to speed on the definition of camp, but I did need a little elucidation on the job description of a purser. So in case you do too, a purser is one who deals with the ships 'purse'. They deal with the hospitality side of the ship, including passenger relations and accountancy and they are usually treated as officers. Along with the chief purser, this was Keith's job. But he also saw his role, having risen through the ranks from storekeeper, to cook, to steward, as guiding all the catering staff and making sure they were as happy as his passengers. He became a big brother to many of the crew on the *Norland* and when I asked him if he could track down Roy/Wendy for me, he went one better, as I came to learn he often has throughout his life. Well, quite a few better actually. In my ignorance I still thought Wendy's war was the whole story, but Keith told me that, as well as Roy and himself, I would be meeting nine other crew members across all departments of the ship. So, never one to look a gift horse in the mouth, without hesitation I booked my ticket to Hull.

I arrive in the bar of the Royal Station Hotel in Hull and spot six grey- to white-haired sixty-something men all chatting away, laughing and joking and I feel like I'm crashing a reunion. Well, I am, sort of. And this festival atmosphere is all thanks to Keith, who is quick to notice me looking lost in the hotel lobby and introduces himself in his softly spoken, genial way.

Whilst Thatcher was dividing the nation with her iron fist in the early 1980s, Keith was binding his team together with kid gloves. So ever since, when Keith asks the crew to get together they jump at the chance: the chance to see their 'family' again, the chance to do anything for Keith, as he always did for them. He introduces me to the others.

John 'Fozzie' Foster, one of the ship's barmen, is pint-sized with pint in hand. A no-nonsense chap with an almost fierce sounding East Yorkshire brogue, which emanated from beneath one of those Tom Selleck moustaches back in the eighties. 'Like a male model he was,' says Wendy about him. However, it doesn't take long before the salty, golden heart is revealed beneath John's tough exterior, as is the case with most of these men.

Frankie Green, steward to the officers, was a loud, ear-ringed, muscular, vest-topped playboy with a perm in the eighties, who's now more like Frankie Howerd, according to Wendy and a little bit like Larry Grayson, according to me, thanks to the glasses which hang on a chain around his neck. 'She was the mother hen of the ship,' Wendy says of Frankie, referring to him, as they do to each other always, in the feminine.

Roy 'Wendy' Gibson him/herself has a touch of John Inman

about him. Perhaps the white hair he has now helps me draw that image rather lazily. Back in 1982 he was sporting a big dark bouffant and, though his voice isn't as booming as Frankie's, he was and is equally and unashamedly camp. So much so that everyone, even the most macho of crew members, refer to him as Wendy. As we begin to talk, three young railway workmen, the epitome of macho, walk through the bar from the station in their luminous overalls and Wendy shouts out to them, 'Oo, the strippers have arrived! We're over 'ere, lads!' The three workmen, more used to wolf-whistling passing girls, no doubt, than being harassed by male pensioners, shrivel with embarrassment and, as I look at Frankie and Wendy fearlessly enjoying themselves, I think about those gay liberationists, those detractors of camp as something that disempowers, and I cannot agree.

Bob Lough, unlike the rest, doesn't have that distinctive 'ull accent. Born in Newcastle, raised in Wales and educated in grammar schools and naval establishments, his father being a sailor too, Bob speaks the Queen's English, and has the poise and the calm you might expect of a Chief Officer (now Captain).

Brian 'Shep' Shepherd on the other hand is an old sea dog. Or as Wendy describes him, 'A big bastard, strong, you know't I mean, and lovely with it.' In 1982 he was already in his early forties, with his oil-black hair slicked back and the skin on his hands as tough as old mooring ropes, having been an able seaman on the *Norland* since her maiden voyage in 1974, and consequently vehemently protective of her.

Also joining us is the theatrical Ray 'Candy' Millington, another of the sea queens who worked as a steward on the *Norland*, but didn't actually go with the crew down to the Falklands. Nevertheless *she,* as it seems only proper to refer to her (as well as refer to Frankie and Wendy, as they all do to each other) regales us that day in the bar with wonderful and sometimes apocryphal tales of life on the ships before and after the war.

On subsequent visits I am introduced to others.

Malcolm 'Mally' Gelder, one of the *Norland*'s cooks, a bright-blue-eyed and gentle figure, slightly nervous about revealing too much of the naughtiness that occurred on board the *Norland* just in case any of it could be construed as criminal these days. His crew mates, however, are quick to reassure him that so much water has passed under the bridge, both metaphorically and literally speaking in their case, that most subjects are fair game now.

Dave Risby, who was one of three second officers (or second mates) on board in 1982. He's the only southerner among the group, an Essex boy in fact, but not, thank God, imbued with that jaw-dropping stupidity and phobia about consonants which phenomena such as TOWIE have left the unfortunate county reeling from, but full of technical information and great anecdotes from the bridge of the ship. Born in Leigh-on-Sea in 1945, he first went to sea, like most of the lads, at the ripe old age of sixteen and, also like most of them, joined the *Norland* when it was launched in 1974.

Brian Lavender is a northerner, but of Ireland. He attended a top grammar school in Northern Ireland, left home at nineteen and spent the next eleven years sailing all over the Far East on tankers. He met his Malaysian wife Liz when sailing for Shell Eastern and they married in her home country in 1968. Mixing with mainly English officers and Chinese crews he has lost many of his Irish idioms, but not his beguiling accent. His mother was an elocution teacher, who 'would have dropped dead if she had heard some of my workmates'. He first arrived in Hull in 1974 just as the newly launched *Norland* was taking applications for a Radio Officer, then sporting massive spectacles so fashionable in the early eighties, no doubt to help him keep an eye on all that coded information spewing from the bank of (by today's standards) oversized, grey radio equipment in the *Norland*'s communications room.

When I tell Wendy I'm staying in the Royal Station hotel tonight, she nods knowingly and says, 'I've stopped here a few times.'

'Doing business!' Frankie cuts in and Wendy shoots him a sidelong glance in the manner of all great double acts, and while I'm trying to contain my laughter Frankie looks at his watch and exclaims, 'Well, sorry burr I've gorra go home and feed pussy, ant I?'

'I've got my pussy to feed un'all,' Wendy counters with a quick purse of the lips in the tradition of all great *Carry On*s.

'I've got two dogs at home,' Candy chimes in.

'Three dogs with yourself,' Frankie adds.

Far from being offended, Candy says, 'Well, as I prefer to say, two dogs and a bitch.'

'*There's* the bitch,' Wendy points at Frankie, and I could watch this show all night.

But it's time to go. As we finish up talking on this first of what will be many glorious meetings with the lads, it has become clear to me that what all these very distinctive characters so clearly share is a passion for their ship and a passion for the story they shared.

So what follows is my attempt, as they talked animatedly to

me and sometimes over each other, to set it all down. Sometimes a transcription and sometimes a retelling of the stories and information they collectively blessed me with; sometimes conflicting in their subjectivity, sometimes hazy through aging memories, but all equally valid, all necessary in portraying, at the very least, a glimpse of what I absorbed, because soon it dawned on me that this is a story of unsung heroes that the world really needs to know.

16 APRIL 1982

Brian Lavender, radio officer on the *Norland* is at his station in the radio room. Garish orange curtains with a geometric pattern are pulled over the windows blocking out the gloom of the mid-April night and the rain, which is topping up the North Sea as the ship steams out of Rotterdam for the twelve-hour trip back to Hull.

Covering the lower half of one of the wood veneer walls is a fat grey panel of buttons and dials, switches and wires looking like something from the Tardis on *Dr Who*, which has just finished its nineteenth series with Peter Davison as the mysterious Time Lord. The most recognisable thing on this panel, to the layman that is, is a dark grey telephone receiver. A black vinyl plaque with GUBH etched in white on it is screwed to the panelling below the clock in the unlikely event that the experienced radio officer would ever need reminding of the ship's call sign as he sits at the desk in his crisp white shirt, gold epaulettes and black tie.

Another quiet evening watch has Brian glancing towards the door there in the office bulkhead and the relative comfort of an officer's cabin waiting for him just behind it. But thoughts of home keep him going for now. By nine in the morning he'll be on his way to the wife and kids.

Then a call from Humber radio snaps him from his reverie. They are using their call sign GKZ on the 500 kHz frequency. Radio operators always keep watch on 500 kHz, the international distress and calling frequency for Morse code. It has a maximum range of about five hundred miles, which is fine for ferries such as the *Norland* as they are never that far from land anyway. The message simply says: 'q t c 1'.

Which means I have one message for you.

Brian and Humber radio transfer to different working frequencies and GKZ sends the message in Morse code. A message addressed to the Master of the ship is soon beeping through. A message from Westminster, from the Department of Trade.

The message is in plain language, just like a letter, but sent in Morse code. It takes about five minutes to receive it.

Brian acknowledges using his Vibroflex Morse code key. It's his very own 'bug', or semi–automatic key, given to him by the US Navy when he served on the merchant fleets in Vietnam in '66. He's carried it from ship to ship ever since as it enables him to communicate at higher speeds than can possibly be obtained with a traditional up/down key. It took him a while to get used to it, but once he mastered it he never looked back.

The signallers finish by wishing each other: 'g n o m' (Good night old man).

Then Brian turns to the white typewriter. Usually he just writes out the messages in long hand, but he reckons this one is worth typing; it sounds like a big deal to him. He makes two copies, one to file and one for the addressee, which he pulls from the typewriter and takes up to the captain's cabin. Captain Ellerby isn't there. Brian asks around until he eventually finds him in the bar enjoying a quiet gin and tonic after his watch with some friends who had boarded in Rotterdam. Brian gives his captain the note and the captain reads it in an instant, a lot quicker than it took Brain to receive it, even with his beloved bug key. Ellerby's face drops. He becomes a little pale. The people he is drinking with have no idea why, but Brian, privy to every message sent to the ship, does.

Ellerby hurries off to find his senior officers: Bob, the chief officer; Lloyd, the chief engineer; and John, the chief purser. And by nine o'clock the following morning, after all passengers and cargo have been safely discharged in Hull, the senior officers have assembled their entire crews in the ship's restaurant for a briefing like no other this company has ever heard.

1

RUM, BUM
AND BACCY

JOHN FOSTER (Ship's Barman)

Hull – 17 April 1982

We was all standing round in the restaurant, looking at each other and muttering, brewing up little rumours about why the Captain had called us all together like this. It rarely happened, I mean, all of us at the same time. Some of us was up in front of him often enough getting a doing for one prank or another, especially the frigging 'girls'. But this was different. It felt different. And Captain Ellerby looked different as he came in and stood by the bar, his usually wide smile all deflated, his eyes fixed on the floor in front of his feet.

Frankie was mincing about, as usual, humming that 'Don't You Want Me, Baby' song that was all over the radio at the time.

I asked Keith, coz he was assistant purser, 'They told you owt?'

'No, nowt,' he goes.

Then Ellerby looked up and we all shushed, keen to hear what the hell was going on.

'You've all heard on the news about the Falklands, no doubt.'

'You mean bloody Malvinas, don't yer?' some sarky bloke whispered near me, but I didn't turn to look who. Too busy studying Ellerby's face, trying to predict what he was going to say before he said it.

'Well, the *Norland*,' he took a deep breath, 'has been requisitioned by the MOD to carry troops down towards the Falklands.'

A murmur went round, and just as I was thinking it, Carol said it out loud: 'And worr about us? Worr'll happen t'our jobs?'

Carol was a stewardess and at close to sixty, with her big peroxide perm, she was the grand old lady of the crew. She had no fear about piping up in front of Captain. Not that Captain Ellerby was someone to be scared of. He was a lovely bloke. But right now there was a sadness in his eyes when he said, 'The *Viking 6* will take over our route from Hull to Rotterdam and there'll be places for you there if you want them. But if you want to stay with the *Norland* – and it's not compulsory, mind you – but if you want to volunteer to transport the troops down to Ascension Island… only to Ascension and then we're coming back…'

'There'll be extra pay?' Bill asked. Being a Union man, he weren't backward in coming forward neither.

'Well, yes there will be a considerable weekly bonus.'

Frankie chimed in, clapping his hands together like a frigging seal, 'And we'll have a ferry-load of strapping squaddies to look after all the way down there?'

Captain nodded, his smile creeping back over his unusually

stubbly face. 'But, like I say, it's volunteers only, no one's making you go.'

It was Ellerby's ship. There was no doubt he was going. But it was our ship too. We had no intention of leaving her. She was as much part of the family as the folk on board her. Where she went, we went.

'So who's in?'

Every hand in the room, without fail, shot up in the air.

16 April 1982   Shipping Policy Division
Mr I. Dunlop   DEPARTMENT OF TRADE
North Sea Ferries B.V.   PARLIAMENT SQUARE HOUSE
Europort   34-36 PARLIAMENT STREET
Beneluxhaven   LONDON SW1A 2ND
Holland

NOTICE OF REQUISITION

The Secretary of State for Trade in exercising the powers conferred upon him by the Requisitioning of Ships Order 1982 hereby requisitions the m.v. "NORLAND" and requires you to place the said vessel at his disposal upon completion of discharge at Hull on Saturday 17th April.

The Master of the said vessel is to be instructed to report to Captain D Sims, the Department of Trade Sea Transport Officer as to destination and employment of the said vessel. Please refer any general enquiries to the above address.

A further letter will be sent to you regarding the charter party arrangements which it is proposed to apply to the m.v. 'NORLAND'.

Designation of Requisitioning Authority
S. S. Holness
Senior Principal
Department of Trade

FRANKIE GREEN (Officers' Steward)

Well, I never did it for Queen and bloody country I can tell you that. I was the only queen I gave a shit about. Me and the other 'girls', especially Wendy, or Roy as he was known to his mam. We had both been stewards on the *Norland* for a few years by then and we loved it. But when we was told she was being commissioned to take paratroopers down to the Falklands – Second Battalion, Parachute Regiment (or 2 Para) to be precise – we was both as excited as a nun at a cucumber stall.

But while we was revelling in the thought of being confined on a ship for weeks on end with nine hundred fit young men standing to attention, so to speak, people back home in Hull started talking, you know, as they do, telling me it was too dangerous to go down there what with the war and that. I remember Judy, she was a shop girl on one of the other North Sea Ferries ships what did the route to Bruges, and she saw me and said, 'Now, Frankie, don't tell me you're on this trip down the Atlantic!'

I said, 'Yeah, 'course I am, love.'

And she said (and this was the night before I was due to sail, you know), 'Don't be ridiculous, it won't come back. That boat int meant for high seas. It's gorra flat bottom for one thing. If you go, you won't be coming back.'

Charming! I thought. What a thing to say to me just before I'm about to get on board. But I just kept thinking of the thousand squaddies that was going to be there too and it softened the blow.

JOHN

I went home and told my parents. I was living with them above the pub they ran at the time, you see, after my first marriage ended in divorce. I had a bairn, a daughter, she was only four at the time, but she lived with her mam. So it was my parents I told first, as we was having our tea.

'Mam, our ferry's been requisitioned. I'm taking troops down towards the Falklands.'

'No you bleeding ent,' she says.

I goes, 'Worra yer talking about?'

And she goes, 'You ent bloody going to no Falklands.'

'I'm thirty-two not frigging sixteen, mam,' I goes, 'You can't be telling me what to do still.'

'As long as you're living under this roof…' she goes until my dad cuts in.

'Lerrim go,' he went, without even dragging his eyes from the telly. I think he was watching *Game for a Laugh* or something like that. *Game for a Laugh* or *Larry Grayson's Generation Game.* It had to be, as it was a Saturday and there was only three channels to choose from at the time. And my dad wouldn't have been watching BBC 2, I can tell you that much. 'Lerrim go for God's sake. Lerrim do what he wants,' he grumbled at me mam, 'he needs to be with his mates.'

He was right. He understood. His father, my grandfather, had been in the Merchant Navy and my dad was on the trawlers himself before he gave it up to become a landlord. We all stuck together on *Norland*. Whoever we was. Whatever our differences. She was our ship. And she was the glue that kept us all together.

DAVE RISBY (Second Officer)

Alan, one of the other second officers (or second mates as we were also known) called me as I was on leave at the time and said, 'Dave, I've got something to ask you. You see, the *Norland*'s been requisitioned…'

'Yeah, I'll go,' I said before he'd even finished his sentence.

It came at the perfect time for me. I was just in the middle of a divorce and I couldn't wait to pack my bags and put a few thousand miles between me and all that malarkey.

BOB LOUGH (Chief Officer)

I think we all saw it as a jolly big adventure, to be honest. We'd all been working for a long time on the North Sea run. There were only two British flagships on it: *Norwave* and *Norland*. It was a nice run, but let's face it, it was just back and forth to Holland, so when the voyage to Ascension came up with *Norland* as a troopship… Well, let's just say, we were all a lot younger and dafter at the time, so we thought we should go.

BRIAN LAVENDER (Radio Officer)

The morning we arrived back in Hull after receiving that telegram from the Department of Trade, the morning the MOD was to take over the *Norland*, was the morning I was due to go on leave for a whole month. It was a wee bit strange leaving the ship at such a pivotal time, but I was going home to my gorgeous Malaysian wife and two young children for a whole month, so I wasn't that bothered. It wasn't like I was leaving the ship without a radio officer, of course. My relieving officer arrived on board as I was on my way.

'How's it going?' I said to him as I begun the handover, 'Everything grand with the missus there?'

'Everything's great,' he says rubbing his tired eyes, 'Apart from the morning sickness what happens morning, noon and night, the mood swings, and the sending me on the road at all hours to buy worrever it is she's craving this time.'

'Oh well, you can have bit of a wee break, so you can, now you're working,' I says and he nods and rolls his eyes, 'Have you got a name for the wee one yet?' I asks.

'She wants Diana, if it's a girl, but me, I'll worry about all that when the bairn is out and everything's in order, you know.'

'Well, good luck to you, buddy, with that, and with your watch for that matter.'

'What do you mean?'

'Thing's might be a little different today,' I told him, 'But I'm sure the Captain will fill you in, when he knows what the hell is going on himself,' and off I went home without a care in the world.

I'd spent a week at home with the family before I got a call from North Sea Ferries saying would I come back to work for the run to Ascension. My relief was not allowed to go after all as the MOD had just told them no civilian was allowed to go if their wife was pregnant.

I had a big discussion with my wife, but we had to make up our minds pretty quickly. In the end we decided I should go. It wasn't the extra money that swung it, though it did help. It was more that it seemed the right thing to do. And personally I have to say there was an element of adventure about it as life on board the ferries can become rather mundane at times, just going back and forth as we did. Besides, we were only going to Ascension, were we not? But then, now I think about it, why was the MOD so worried about husbands of pregnant wives going only to Ascension Island?

ROY 'WENDY' GIBSON (Steward)

I didn't think twice about going to Ascension. I didn't! And it was not just coz of all those fit squaddies what was on board. Worrit was, we was family on the *Norland*. A little floating village, you know't I mean? It had been that way for a good few years before the Falklands. We did the route from Hull to Rotterdam. Eight days on, eight days off. Frankie looked after the officers up on A Deck and we (Carol, Candy, me and the other stewards and stewardesses) looked after the passengers on D Deck, serving in the restaurant or doing their rooms, changing sheets and all that. We worked two shifts a day. From five thirty in the morning doing the breakfasts and what not till lunchtime. Then we'd get into our civvies and do our own thing until we was back on at four o'clock in the afternoon until ten in the evening. After that we liked to let our hair down. And sometimes we wouldn't even get any sleep before we started again in morning. Candy was the worst for that. Always hung over she was.

Well, worrit was, Candy was a bloke, you see. Real name Ray Millington. Candy and me we had this drag act back in Hull and we'd dock at eleven in morning after our eight days on and by half past nine that night we'd be in fishnets and feathers on stage playing the pubs and clubs every night till it was time to sign back on to *Norland* again. I played piano so I'd accompany Candy who did all the banter and jokes. And also she was a mime act, you know't I mean, miming the words to songs on tape. And I'd operate the tapes for her sometimes. Most of the time I wasn't in drag, but I'd be like Liberace. I had some lovely jackets with rhinestones and sequins on them and that felt better than having all the make-up and dresses on when I was jumping up and down playing as fast as you like and getting everyone up dancing, coz I'd be sweating buckets. Like a bleeding colander I was. So most times I just wore a birrof eye-liner and mascara, not all the slap, you know't I mean? And I could never find a nice pair of ladies shoes anyway, coz I had size twelve feet so I had to settle for a pair of flip flops and decorate them with a birra tinsel. I was jealous of all the other queens who could slip on a nice pair of heels.

FRANKIE

Oo yeah. Like Candy, you mean? Well, she was always a state in morning. Drunk or fooking sober, energy was never her thing. Half the time she'd be sitting there with her head in her hands going, 'Oo,' she said, 'Francis,' she said, 'You couldn't do us a few bunks, could yer? I'm too tired to be changing beds now. Me 'ed is so dreadful.'

So me being the good friend what I was, I goes, 'OK, love, you take it easy.' And me and Wendy and the rest got on with doing the cabins, until I hear Candy squealing with delight. She's down in one of the other cabins and she's found a pair of high heeled shoes what some passenger had left behind, you know, and what fitted her. Well, these high heels was like magic bloody slippers to Candy, let me tell you, whose aches and pains seemed to have vanished and she came skipping down the corridor in these fooking shoes going, 'Look worr I found, Look worr I found!'

'Well, I'm very happy for you, love,' I goes, 'But if you think I'm doing any more bunks for you, you've got another fooking thing coming.'

WENDY

I might've had trouble finding ladies shoes to fit, but I remember having a good crack at the rest of the outfit on many an occasion, if me, Frankie and Candy was out on the piss. Like the time we went out as St. Trinian's girls. I had the pigtails and the tennis racket and the slap on.

FRANKIE

And one of your testicles was hanging out your knickers, wunt it?

WENDY

Oo, yeah, it was. One of my ovaries was hanging out and I didn't realise till someone asked me worrit was dangling there.

Anyway, once a month, after work, we had a drag night in the crew mess un'all. Candy and me, we would do the show and everyone would come. I brought my grandma's old piano on board for it. I painted it bright pink and I'd slip on a nice dress from C&A. I was always nice and slim back then, helped by the slimming pills I'd get from my Indian G.P. He was a lovely man. Got me worrever I needed as long as I brought him his cigarettes and whiskey back from the Duty Free shop on the ship.

Anyway, worrit was, for these drag nights we'd make it all nice with candles on the tables and that, and we'd invite passengers too. The factory girls would come down, what was off on a jolly to Holland because the factories had closed for the two weeks in the summer, so the straight men was happy. And us queens was happy coz all the lorry drivers on the freight runs would come down too. It got to the point that the crew bar was making more money on these nights than any other bar on the ship.

Everyone was having such a good time and frankly I think one of my bosses, who shall remain nameless, got a bit jealous coz he put a stop to it. He didn't know if he was a Martha or an Arthur that one. He used to call me Margaret Lockwood, you know, the actress on account of my black hair, thick like an Italian it was. I think he fancied me, but he couldn't say anything, so far in the closet, you know't I mean? There's nothing worse than a black market queen at sea.

Anyway, like I say, I played everything and anything. Ragtime, sing-a-long, classical, ballads, worrever they wanted. I have this knack of being able to hear something once and then I can play it. By ear, you know't I mean? When I was a kid I used to go to Mrs Pratt for lessons. Oo, what a state she was, lipstick up to her nose and that. But worrit was, she said eventually she was wasting her time teaching me, as well as wasting my dad's money, coz I was putting too many fiddly bits in the pieces she was showing me. I was better than her, you see!

But I didn't always play with Candy. Sometimes she was on one side of town doing her thing and I did my own thing on the other. My haunts were Spring Bank, Beverley Road and the Old Town.

JOHN

He played at my father's pub The Yorkshireman un'all, doing background music for the dominoes club on a Sunday, dint yer?

WENDY

I did. It was a nice family atmosphere in there. That was a far cry from clubs like St. Andrews. Oo, my God that was rough. And the first time I went there all the punters did was eff and blind at me as I played. Well, in the end the only thing I could do was eff and blind back at them. And instead of braying me head in, which they could've, they loved it and I had them eating out my hand by the end of the show.

The landlord said to me after, 'You gave 'em their own medicine, Wendy, and that's what they like in 'ere.'

I didn't play a lot of gay bars, believe it or not because I can't be doing with a load of Marys. They get on me bastard nerves most of the time. And worrit was, this was the seventies and people would spit at you in street if they knew you was gay. Once outside a pub on Hessle Road – they was rough bastards round there – Candy got bashed in the face with a bottle. The bottle didn't smash, but it broke her bloody nose. Blood streaming down her face. Just coz she was a poof.

FRANKIE

But that weren't coz she was gay, love, that was coz she was a shit cabaret artist!

No, but seriously, back on *Norland* there was never any of that terrible gay bashing you got on the streets. It was another world. Especially if Keith was on. And Captain Ellerby, he was a pleasure to look after.

WENDY

Yes. If Keith was assistant purser on our run I'd be happy as Larry.

KEITH (Assistant Purser)

Candy used to come and wake everybody up for work at five in the morning. Probably coz she hadn't been to bed herself yet. I might have been an officer, but it didn't stop her rapping on my door and shouting: 'Keith, love, are you up yet?'

I'd mumble something into my pillow and she'd knock again going, 'Keith, if you don't gerrup, I'm gerrin in.'

Well, that did the trick every time, I can tell you. I was up like a shot.

Then when I was up and about I'd find her sitting on one of the draining boards in the pantry soaking her sore feet in the sink…

FRANKIE

From all those fooking magic slippers!

KEITH

Aye, and one of the other 'girls', probably Mimi, sitting on the other draining board with her feet in the other sink. And a bottle of Bacardi in the middle for them to share. But I never had a go at them unnecessarily, like, because it was actually bloody hard work being a steward on them ships back then. I know coz I'd done the job myself (I'd been storekeeper, cook and steward on the *Norland* from 1974 when she was first launched). They needed a release, you see, the crew, and as long as they didn't tekk the piss I lerrem have it.

I had to laff though coz later on you'd see them serving breakfasts in the restaurants still with their nail varnish and make-up on.

WENDY

Well, we hadn't had time to gerrit all off, had we? So like Keith says, there we was, with the passengers raising their eyebrows as we handed them their full English with red finger-nails, and us looking back at them with eyes like Dusty Springfield.

KEITH

One morning one of the passengers came up to me in the restaurant and started ranting at me, 'It's bloody disgusting!'

I said, 'What, madam?'

She goes, 'There's a bloke there serving food and he's full of cold. He shouldn't be working around the food.'

I went over to see who she was referring to and it was just one of the alcoholic staff shivering with DTs, not with cold at all. There was a fair bit of drinking went on on them ships, I have to say. Must have been all the duty free.

WENDY

Mimi and Candy was having a drink after work one night out on deck and the purser came rushing by saying, 'There's a load of deck chairs out on deck aft. Go and stack 'em up for us, there's good lads.'

Well, worrit was, never one to make unnecessary work for herself, and coz she'd had a drink on her, Candy marches to the after end and chucks all these deck chairs overboard, so there'd be none to stack in future, you know't I mean? So there was a trail of these bloody chairs bobbing along on the waves all the way from Rotterdam to Hull.

Some of the crew accommodations was five flights below on G deck, well under the water line. If that ship had ever sunk we would have been the first to gerrit. And our cabins was directly below the freight deck too so that when we went down after breakfast the air was blue with diesel fumes. We spent a lot of time coughing down there.

FRANKIE

Nothing to do with the all the cigarettes, of course, love.

WENDY

But in winter we could do our eight days on the ship and never see daylight. Coz we'd come up from G Deck at 05:30 and it would still be dark by the time we were finishing up breakfasts and going down to our cabins again. And the same in evening when we came up at 4:00pm to do the evening shift.

FRANKIE

If it weren't for all the cock, we wouldn't have purrup wirrit!

The captain was always great to work for, but I still couldn't resist tekkin the piss now and then. One of my jobs was: in the afternoon go up for'ard to Captain's cabin and deliver his tea tray. Then give him an hour or so, so he could have his nap and all the rest of it, before going back to retrieve his tray. At which point I knock on the door and I say, 'All right, Captain, I'll just go through to the bedroom and remake your bed before I take the tray.'

'Thank you, Francis,' he says, sat in his day room at the mirror, doing his tie and what not.'

So I goes into his room, shut the door behind me and go about making his big double bed (not like our little single bunks), washing down his basin and shower, a good quarter of an hour's work, you know. And as I'm finishing up and going back out into his day room I was surprised to see his family and friends had come on board while we were docked, and they was all sitting around there with him chatting and what not. Now, I don't know what came over me, but as everyone turns to see me coming out of his bedroom I pretend I'm all sleepy and go, 'Oo, Captain, I wish you'd woken me earlier, love.'

Well, his face drained. As did his wife's, as I grabbed the empty tea tray and floated on out.

BRIAN

When you joined a ship you signed on the ship's articles, by which I mean a contract of work. There were two types of article: Foreign Going and Home Trade (including the near continent). Ferries fell into the second category. Ships complements also fell into two types: the Officers and the crew. The officers consisted of the deck officers (Captain otherwise known as Master, Chief Officer, Second Officer, Third Officer and the Radio Officer, which was me); and the engineer officers (chief engineer, second engineer, third engineer, and petty officer motormen in the *Norland*'s case). The crew were also split into deck, engine and catering. The catering department was headed up by the chief steward (or Purser on the passenger ships), who was also classed as an officer; then there were the cabin stewards, cooks, storemen and so forth down to the galley boy.

The officers and crew were pretty much separate entities and, although they worked together, they did not normally mix together socially on the ship. That was just the way it was.

WENDY

Oo, yes, it was like *Upstairs, Downstairs* on them ships. And we was most definitely downstairs.

FRANKIE

If you know what she means!

WENDY

Well the officers worked and lived pretty much on A Deck and we was working three decks below on D Deck, as well as living on G Deck, in the bowels of the ship.

FRANKIE

And it smelt like the bowels too at times, let me tell you. I had the biggest cabin coz it was on the corner, but it was also the noisiest, right above the engine room, I was. I got so used to the noise that to this day I cannot sleep in silence. I have to have the telly going or the radio on. And back in '79 when there was so much talk about the Yorkshire Ripper – when he had supposedly sent that tape to George Oldfield, the detective in charge of the investigation, what went in that spooky voice, 'They never learn do they, George?' – my cabin was full of mattresses with four or five queens crammed in going 'Shift up,' all convinced the fooking Ripper was on board. Well, you never know, some of them lorry drivers going to and fro looked fooking dodgy enough. And then Kempy, he was one of the other stewards, made it worse by calling down the alleyway in that same spooky voice what was on the tape, 'You'll never learn, girls, you'll never learn!' Well, that did it, dint it, we was all climbing over each other trying to get furthest from the door in this fooking cabin of mine convinced he was coming to gerrus. And he was bound to be after me first, wuntee, what wimme being so bonnie.

WENDY

Oo, here she goes!

BRIAN

As I was saying, the officers had their own mess room (or saloon) for eating, and recreation room for relaxing. It included a bar, dart board, a wee library and easy chairs. It was also known as the smoke room. Usually this was the place we met after *watch* (ie a shift), had a drink and generally relaxed. In the bigger traditional companies the saloon was quite formal: you had to be in uniform for meals, tables were laid with white starched tablecloths and starched linen napkins with the ring engraved with your rank; you always sat in the same place with the captain at the head of the table. In my early days I sailed mainly with Chinese and Indian crews, later Filipinos. There were usually two or three stewards serving in the saloon at meal times. The food was very good and varied.

The crew ate in their own mess room which was more informal, but they had their own rec room as well. The officers had their own private cabins with bathroom, shower and loo. The crew tended to share a cabin, but not on the *Norland*, unless they were hiding from the bloody Yorkshire Ripper of course!

Most officers in the end, after maybe ten years service, came into Home Trade ships, i.e. ferries. They got fed up with long trips away from home. For example, only my second trip working was two years away without leave. Ferries gave you more money, more time off and a home life. Most ferries in the seventies were British crewed. Most of the officers were ex deep sea. That wasn't always the case with the crew, but the separation was the same; we didn't really mix socially.

Frankie was a steward in the officers' mess on the *Norland*. He was, how shall we say, a bit of a character, but we usually only saw him at meal times. He was very camp and his favourite phrase to the fresh faced junior officers when chicken was on the menu was…

FRANKIE

'Would you like stuffing, sir?'

BRIAN

Not very original, perhaps, but it always raised a laugh.

FRANKIE

It raised more than that in some cases, I can tell you.

BRIAN

Wendy was a steward for the crew and so we officers saw him even less, but he had a great reputation for playing the piano in the crew mess and singing a few songs. Although we didn't mix socially on board, once ashore in a foreign port we would drink together and get on just fine. And not only did we drink together, Wendy would be playing the piano in the bars in Holland too.

WENDY

Well, worrit was, I would clock off the ship at noon and by one o'clock in the afternoon, after I'd had a spot of lunch, I'd be playing the piano in the Amstel Bar in Europort, Rotterdam. The landlady there was called Anna. Lovely lady. And I couldn't get enough of playing the piano. It was my escape from everything in a way. I was a member of the Artists' Federation by then. I had joined in 1981, but I didn't ask for paying when I played for Anna. Although I did get free Bacardis all afternoon, which was nice. It was dead popular that place. Anna made so much money she had the place extended. I knew loads of people from Holland. I knew Amsterdam better than I knew Hull. Frankie's second home was Rotterdam. Some of the lads from the *Norland* would be there in Europort too, drinking in the beer garden, or playing pool, while the others would go and play football at the seaman's mission. Sailors from all over, from all the different ships would be there drinking and socialising.

FRANKIE
And what not!

WENDY
I'd play till three then I'd be back on the ship for my shift what started at four in the afternoon, unless it was winter. In the winter we barely left the ship. We couldn't be bothered. It was too bleeding cold, you know't I mean?

FRANKIE
Depends who you had to keep you warm, love!

WENDY
We worked hard on that ship. We worked hard and we played hard. But the next morning, if we'd partied all night in the crew mess, even though I was aching so much I'd be walking like a Whitby crab, I was still there on time to do my job and do it well.
  I loved it. We all did. The fun that we had!

FRANKIE

It didn't stop you disappearing that time though, did it?

WENDY

Well, worrit was, around '76, '77 before I started on the *Norland* I was a steward on the oil rigs down near Yarmouth. The money was good burr it was such a homophobic bloody place. Nowt like the Merchant Navy. There's some right wankers on them rigs, real hard cases, you know't I mean? And I needed more money to keep up the HP payments on the furniture. I was living with me mam at the time and she wouldn't have us out of work. Ever. She wanted her board and lodging money on the mantelpiece every week. So I wrote to North Sea Ferries and managed to get a summer season on *Norland* and keep my job on the rigs too. Well, they liked me on the rigs. My boss there said, 'Don't leave us, Roy,' he said, 'You always do such a good job.' So I did go back to the rigs, but I had such good summers on the ships. I suddenly had a social life, a home life, and better paid work. I didn't know you could actually have a job where you could drink too, coz that wasn't allowed on the rigs. And I didn't have to put up with any more shite from all the homophobes there. On the ships you were accepted more. I s'pose you had to be in a way. The crew was out on our route for eight days at a time without a break. On other ships cruises went on for weeks, if not months if you was going down to Australia or worrever. While you was out at sea it was a world of its own, away from normal life, away from life back in England, where you was spat at in the street, or worse, for being a Mary. There was no head bangers on a ship. And no police neither. I s'pose the straight men in the crew was more open-minded coz they had travelled all over the world.

FRANKIE

And because some of them was half-poofs. I mean, coz there was hardly any women on board ships in them days, sometimes the straight men decided to have a bit of cock just while they was away at sea, you know, and when they got back to shore they'd go back to their wives and girlfriends as if nowt had happened.

WENDY

And because we all had to work as a team when you're out on a ship in the middle of the ocean for however long. You can't afford not to get along coz there's nowhere to go if you don't, you know't I mean? It was live and let live there. And besides, the bosses of the shipping companies actually wanted queens to work on the hospitality side, as stewards and that, because we was so bloody good at it. It was all about the attention to detail, the cleanliness, them nice little touches to the service that the straight blokes what was stewards mightn't bother with. The queens was always immaculately turned out and the officers loved that, coz the passengers loved it; they loved a quality service, you see. Most of us worked bloody hard and grafters are what matter on a ship. Hard grafters are welcome, whatever their preference, you know't I mean? And the passengers liked a bit of camp too coz it was entertaining for 'em. They liked us mincing around and making a fuss of 'em.

KEITH

Some of the passengers would actually ask us when they was booking a table who the waiter might be.

'Is it one of the gay boys?' They'd go, 'Oh, I do hope so, because we always have someone who's gay. We had Diamond Lil last time.'

WENDY

Oo yeah, we all had our regulars on the ship, regular passengers who would come looking for us when they came on.

Worrit was, you wouldn't believe it but sometimes there was more queens than straight folk on them ships. In the crew, I mean. So we could just be ourselves there. I shurr've never looked back after that first summer season on *Norland*, but funnily enough, I did.

Instead of chucking in the rigs I was thinking about leaving Hull altogether and moving to Yarmouth. Things weren't great at home with me mam, you see. I had come home one night after playing a club with Candy. Me mam had been at the club watching, you know't I mean, and she had seen this old queen come up chatting to me asking me if I knew this or that song and it had got her thinking, I s'pose, and she just came out wirrit and went, ''Ere, Roy, do you like men?'

I said, 'Do I like men? I bloody love 'em, mam!'

And without hesitation she snapped, 'Well, you're out the house in morning then.'

That's when I decided, well I might as well bugger off to Yarmouth then.

But you have to understand how hard it was to have a son what was a Mary in them days. I was living with me mam, my step-father Barry and my twin brother. My real dad was a tree feller, a docker and was in the TA. My brother was a rugby player. They couldn't be more bloody butch really, compared to me. But Barry, my step-father, he worked on the ships too as an AB (able seaman) or sometimes the bosun, so he knew from day one I was gay, because he was so used to being around gay blokes. He'd worked among 'em all his life, you know't I mean? So he never had a problem wirrit, but, you know what, apart from me mam that time, all my family was so good about it. And they all loved me to bits.

FRANKIE

Yeah, burr I remember that time. I went to sign back on *Norland*, after my leave, you know, and I saw Carol and I says to her, 'Where's Wendy?'

And she says, 'She's hasn't come back. She's not coming back apparently.'

'Well that don't ring true, do it,' I goes, 'coz I remember her saying only last week how much she loved it on here.'

And she did, just like she said.

Well, I'm not having that, I thought, and I marched off with Carol to look for her. Well, eventually we found her in the market at that old queen's stall who used to go down to London and buy forty-fives what had been on the juke boxes and sell 'em up here dirt cheap. Wendy was buying some records there and I tapped her on the shoulder and goes:

'Wendy, why aren't you back, love?' I said.

'Well, I've chucked it, ant I. I was going to go back to Yarmouth on rigs,' she goes.

'What on earth for?' I asked.

And she goes, 'Oh, I dunno really. Family troubles, I s'pose.'

'But *we're* your family, love,' I said.

'But it's not as secure on the ships, is it?' she says, 'I can't just be living on summer seasons with nothing else for the rest of the year.'

So I goes, 'But purser wants you back for good, he says, coz you're always so immaculately turned out and that.'

It was true un'all. Coz not all the stewards were as professional as Wendy, you see. There was some right mucky buggers on them ferries, unkempt, unshaven, you know. And if a passenger pays good money they want a good service, especially when someone's serving their food.

Then Carol pipes up, 'And we've all got an hour to get back to the ship otherwise we'll all be out a job. Now you coming or what?'

So we marched Wendy back to her mam's, she packed a bag, called up the rigs, told them she wasn't coming back and that was it. She came back to us on *Norland* and everything was hunky dory, just like before.

Until that day in April '82 when nothing was ever the fooking same again.

2

WHO'S THE POOF ON THE PIANO?

BOB

As soon as the *Norland* was requisitioned it went into King George Dock in Hull for a major refit. After all, it was only designed to ferry tourists on an overnight trip across to the Netherlands, not carry troops and military hardware to the other end of the earth. However, the gossip about her being flat bottomed and therefore not fit for the waters of the South Atlantic were not founded. She was a proper ocean-going vessel. North Sea or South Atlantic I knew she'd be fine. But she was not equipped to have helicopters land on her and did not have the kind of secure global communications gear necessary for a ship carrying paratroopers and RAF 18 Squadron heading out on a sabre-rattling exercise to scare the Argentinians back to their mainland.

So the ship was fitted with two Sea King helicopter decks, one aft, one amidships and the fuel capacity had to be increased considerably to give her a range of thirty-two days steaming, which would enable her to travel direct from Portsmouth to the South Atlantic without refuelling. This was achieved by using the ships' ballast tanks. These were cleaned and converted to carry fuel, giving us an extra thousand tonnes capacity. Fresh water capacity had to be increased greatly too, so a desalination plant (or reverse osmosis machine) to convert sea water to fresh, was installed. However, all the available membranes in Europe for the machine had already been snapped up by other ships in the Task Force. You see, we weren't the only STUFT, far from it. STUFT, by the way, stands for *ship taken up from trade*.

FRANKIE

STUFT? More like stuffed, as we was soon to fooking find out, wunt we?

BOB

Well, there were many ships being requisitioned in those weeks. Around fifty merchant ships, I believe, were eventually taken up to support the Task Force for what was being called Operation Corporate, actually outnumbering the Royal Navy vessels. Hence our difficulty locating a membrane for the reverse osmosis machine. However, one was soon located and flown in from Japan to Hull in twenty hours flat, and at huge expense.

After six million pounds were spent on the *Norland* in the space of ten days, it got me thinking whether it was ever really intended to be merely a sabre rattling exercise.

WENDY

After that meeting in the ship's restaurant I went home and told me mam I was off to the Falklands, or to Ascension Island at least. She filled up when I told her. She hadn't chucked me out like she said she was going to. Worrit was, she'd had a drink on her that night. Things always got a bit heated when we'd had a drink on us. The morning after she had called me down for my full English and never said another word about it. In fact she always stood by me. She even slapped a few skate gobs in the face when they threatened to bray us up at some of the rougher places if she was in the audience, you know't I mean?

She was upset, God love her, when I told her I was going down to the South Atlantic, but we needed the money. They was offering us a big bonus for every week we was down there so I could hardly refuse.

FRANKIE

Candy had got another job by then somewhere else. And when we told her that we was all going down to Ascension Island with a thousand fit squaddies she nearly choked. She ran as fast as her little high heels would carry her all the way to the personnel office and asked to be signed back on to *Norland*. But they said they was full up. She wasn't needed. She was fooking gutted.

WENDY

The pink piano I used to play in the crew mess, well, I'd played it so hard for so many years I'd wore it out. So we'd buried it at sea. And before we left for Ascension I asked the Port Chaplain, Reverend Andrews if we could borrow the piano from the mission, just until we got back.

'Of course,' he smiled, God love him, 'As long as you bring it back in one piece and the Argentinians don't kidnap it.'

'Oh no chance of that, Reverend,' I went, 'We're not going anywhere near the Argies.'

Little did I bleeding know!

I just had a little mallam streak in my hair the day we left for Ascension. Just a little streak of grey, you know. Distinguished, like. Within six months I'd gone completely white. Completely white! I bleeding did!

KEITH

When I told my partner Jayne I was off to the South Atlantic she was absolutely fine wirrit. Well, there was no need to worry coz we was only going down to Ascension and we'd only be gone a couple of weeks. But it still didn't stop me feeling awful when I saw my two daughters, they was only five and eight at the time, waving me off on the quayside with their little union jacks.

JOHN

All our families turned out on the dock to wave us off. There was flags being waved, streamers and balloons everywhere. A brass band playing *Rule Britannia* and *Don't Cry for me Argentina* on the quayside and frigging Wendy playing piano on the arse end of the ship. But it was just another job as far as we was concerned. There was no troops on board at the time, you see, apart from a few army and navy officers doing some of the organising with Keith, Bob, Captain Ellerby and the other *Norland* officers. It felt like we was going on a little holiday, with pay.

KEITH

After the refit, *Norland* sailed round from Hull to Portsmouth to load up with troops, artillery and supplies.

Chris Sutcliffe, the storekeeper was put in charge of provisions. We was told we would need to get enough food on board to feed a thousand troops three times a day for sixty days. And there had to be tons of protein to build the troops strength and tons of salads to keep them healthy. George Rimmer was the chief cook and took on the huge responsibility of catering them three thousand meals a day along with his team of cooks, alternating the menu daily as best he could with worree was supplied with. George was a big man. Would have made a good rugby player, but he had a lovely manner. A good ship mate and friend, he was.

Anyway, our normal store rooms were just not big enough for all of those supplies, so me and Chris, along with a gang of navy lads, had container after container transported onto the car deck. Some refrigerated, some not, and we had to make sure we knew exactly what was in which one so we could find what we needed when we needed it in the middle of the bloody ocean.

'Between you and me, Keith,' said the army medic I had to work with in devising the diet for the soldiers, 'Colonel Jones is convinced his boys are going to be suffering with food poisoning and totally out of shape by the time they get to the Falklands. It's your job to prove him wrong.'

No pressure then.

MALCOLM 'MALLY' GELDER (Ship's Cook)
I was used to cooking for large numbers. So was George and the rest of us cooks. The *Norland* could take a maximum of twelve hundred passengers, and back in them days it was like a set menu, all inclusive.

WENDY

Oo, don't remind me! It was a self-service restaurant but we had to clear the tables after 'em. And some of them lorry drivers from the Continent was greedy bastards. They used to stomp into the restaurant at half past nine when we was closing at ten o'clock. And they'd be so pissed they'd be eating off the trays instead of the plates. And the English ladies would be there in their dresses, coz back then they used to get dressed up for dinner. They might have only been cheap glad rags from C&A or worrever, but they made an effort, you know't I mean? They used to love the sense of occasion and we'd make a right fuss of them so they felt special. Burr at the same time these arsehole lorry drivers are delving in the coleslaw with their hands, like pigs they was. Some of the punters, the families, you know, complained about them so I had some of them chucked out a few times. I've never seen so much food wasted.

But there was no way we could let anything go to waste on *this* trip.

MALLY

Burr it was freshness that was a problem on the way down the Atlantic. Just back and forth to Rotterdam we could always pick up fresh ingredients, but the only time we'd be able to stop for fresh stores in the eleven days it took to get to Ascension was at Freetown in Sierra Leone. Some of the shipping containers was refrigerated and we was meant to leave what was in there until last. We had a map drawn up of the containers and what was in each, otherwise we would never have found our way round them; it was like a city in itself down there on the car deck.

DAVE

Everything had been done so fast that as we rounded the coast on the way into Portsmouth there were welders on A Deck still welding the helicopter decks into place. So flames were flashing from their tools, sparks flying, and people were calling me up, as I was on watch, calling from other ships we passed asking, 'Have you got a fire on your ship? Do you need assistance?'

'No, no,' I said, 'But I can't tell you what's going on, top secret and all that.'

As we got into the port we started mooring the ship as we usually do, with thick mooring wires and ropes. Essentially once we had the big insurance wire tied up off the stern of the ship we were good. However, this officious bugger from the navy base comes strutting up and down the dock shouting, 'Send more ropes over, come on! Another rope here. Another rope there!'

I leaned over the side and said, "Ey! Where's the hurricane, mate?'

I mean, we'd run out of ropes to throw him and still he was banging on about moorings. The welders needn't have bothered with the helicopter decks, you could've landed a Chinook on this idiot's hat.

KEITH

The day we got to Portsmouth our Navy counterparts, what was coming down on *Norland* with us, had laid on a little bar in Nelson's old ship HMS *Victory* which was a museum piece by then in Portsmouth harbour. Never afraid of having a good time, half the crew, including the 'girls', ended up drinking the place dry. Then we was delivered back to the hotel in Portsmouth in a big navy truck, which, when it came to an abrupt stop outside, the back dropped open and we all fell out onto the road at the feet of the army officers waiting for us. I looked at them apologetically. They looked at us with, 'What the hell have we got ourselves into?' written all over their faces.

WENDY

Portsmouth – 26 April 1982

Well, worrit was, after that drinking session on board Nelson's ship I was more than ready to oblige if I heard 'Kiss me Hardy,' you know't I mean? So, as I boarded *Norland* at Portsmouth, I went strutting down the corridors, what was teeming with soldiers by now, and I was waving my nail varnished hands at all the squaddies and saying 'Hello darling,' whenever I caught one of 'em staring. Well, the corridor broke out into wolf whistles and jeers and cheers. Some of them shouted nasty things, 'Mind yer backs, lads,' 'Fucking turd burglar,' 'Dirty shirt lifter,' and other little gems like that. Well, I've had to deal with worse growing up in Hull in the seventies, ant I, so it was all water off a duck's back, you know't I mean? I just waved and gorron with it. Gorron with my job. They might not be going on their holidays to Holland like the ladies in their C&A evening dresses, I thought, but I'll look after them as good as I would any tourist. If they don't bloody lynch me first. This was early eighties, you see. You wasn't even allowed to join the army in them days if you was gay.

FRANKIE

Well, at Portsmouth all the troops got a big send off from their families and well-wishers on the dock, waving their fooking Union Jacks and all that, just like we had back up in Hull. 2 Para had their own band and it played on the for'ard deck as the

Norland pulled away. The band was all in their smart uniforms, you know, but two of the drummers, their job was to wear leopard print tunics so long they looked like dresses and wave these frilly things that looked like feather dusters about, like a baton twirler, you see, and I thought, Oo, how camp is that?! And they've got the nerve to tekk the piss out of us for being poofters!

KEITH

Early on in the journey one of the paratroopers asked me if I was gay when he saw Wendy giving me a hug outside the ship's restaurant. I can't remember why Wendy did it. I think perhaps I had given him the afternoon off or something. He was looking a bit frazzled. I was his manager and as far as I was concerned it was my job to make sure my staff was happy. And if they looked like they needed a break I'd step up and muck in. I wasn't trying to be popular. I just believed, and still do, that that's good management.

Anyway, when this Para saw Wendy give me a hug he sneered, 'Are you gay?'

'No,' I said.

'Then why did you let him touch you up like that?'

'Funny,' I said, 'it felt like a hug to me, you know, affection?'

The soldier didn't seem to have a clue what I was talking about, poor bastard.

BRIAN 'SHEP' SHEPHERD (Able Seaman)

When we left Portsmouth with the troops things got, let's say, complicated. We no longer had one captain and one crew, you see. There was us and there was the navy crew, NP1850 (Naval Party 1850), worrad been purron board to accompany us down. I didn't mind having all those soldiers on board: after all, when I needed manpower for some job or t'other I had more hands than I could wish for. But the navy crew came with their own captain and their own buffer (basically the naval equivalent of a bosun), a mad little prick who approached me on my patch the first day and said, 'OK, stand down, fella, I'm in charge down here now.'

'You what?' I goes.

'You heard,' he says.

So I says, 'I tell you what, mate. Do us a favour and work out for me how much sea time you've clocked up in your career, would yer?'

I could see cogs working in his head straight away, but before he opened his gob I added, 'I mean actual sea time, not time spent in barracks or in navy college. *Sea* time. And I'll do same.'

He came back to me a few minutes later, puffing out his chest and announced proudly, 'Two and a half years. Of *actual* sea time. Two and half years.'

'Two and half year, really?' I go.

He nods all proud of it, like.

So I go, 'Well I've got twenty-seven years so fuck off,' I said.

And he did.

The officers were the same, at first. I passed through their bar on my rounds one afternoon. Army and navy officers. About twelve of them there was. They was watching blue movies, you know, as you do and as I passed through one of them tried throwing rank on me and barked, 'Oi, this is an officers' bar, I want you out.'

So I held up this enormous bunch of keys I always had on me. As one of the ship's carpenters I had to have access to all areas for repairs and such, and I goes, 'The only place on this ship I can't go is in Captain Ellerby's day room, so don't tell me where I can go and where I can't go. You're a guest on *my* ship.

I don't care what rank you've got. You're a guest on my ship. Treat me accordingly.'

He shut up pretty sharpish after I said that.

The officers was the worst. The rest of us quickly started mixing, but the army and navy officers couldn't seem to leave their rank outside the door. We'd say 'Come and have a game of darts, but leave your badges in your cabin. Don't be saying I'm a captain so I should be doing this that or the other.' I'd never come across that before. On the merchant ships like *Norland*, we all did our work and respected our bosses, but at the end of the day we was all the same. When you're away at sea for long periods of time it's not a job anymore, it's your life, and we all had to get along together.

There was a lot of jockeying for position on board in the early days. But most of the Paras was right out of their comfort zone. One of the Toms (as they called the privates) comes up to me one day looking a bit green around the gills and said, ''Ere, Shep,' Everyone called me Shep coz me last name is Shepherd, 'Shep,' he says, 'How far are we from land?'

'About five miles.'

'Where? I can't see it,' he goes looking all around.

I went, 'Down there,' pointing through the deck to the seabed.

He thought about what I'd said for a moment then grabbed at the railings going, 'Oh you've just done my head in, you have. You've just right done my head in!'

'What do you mean?' I said a bit mischievous, like.

'You spend all your working life knowing that there's five mile of water between you and the bottom?'

'Well, it's my way of life,' I said, 'You spend all day jumping out of perfectly good airplanes and killing people. That's not my style.'

The Tom couldn't argue with that and we all got on a lot better for those sorts of conversations.

DAVE

A lot of the soldiers were getting sea sick and throwing up at first, but they should have thought themselves lucky they weren't on one of the other merchant ships, or the warships for that matter. Our main advantage over the other older ships was that we had gyro stabilizers. It's a gismo that responds to the roll of the ship and counteracts it by putting out these stabilizing fins from the hull, which means if you're trying to walk around the decks you can do so without looking drunk or if you're trying to eat a meal in the restaurant you can do so without your plate flying off the table. So when we were heading for the Falklands with nothing to stop the wind, which comes hurtling round the tip of South America, and it was blowing a force eight, you could see the Royal Navy ships were rolling their guts out, as was the Europic Ferry (a 4,200-tonne car ferry also requisitioned to carry fuel, ammunition, vehicles and helicopters), but we were steady as a rock. The only thing was the stabilizer worked better if we were going fast, so when we got the call from the fleet commander:

'Reduce speed to nine knots.'

We'd say, 'Nah, we'll stick to twelve, thank you!'

JOHN

I was barman in the For'ard Lounge on *Norland* which became the sergeants' bar when the troops embarked. I thought us lot in the crew was a bunch of nutters, but these sergeants was a right frigging rowdy bunch, to put it mildly. And I hear the Toms, who had their bar on the deck below in the Continental Bar, was even worse. I don't know how we didn't run out of booze. They was pissed as farts most nights, despite there being a ration of three or four beers per night, which they all had chits for. They'd be singing their dirty camp-fire songs, throwing their fists at each other and playing dodgy games.

Apart from a bunch of about twelve soldiers what sat all quiet and moody on the other side of the bar, completely separate from the sergeants. Occasionally, one of them would come up to the bar and say, 'Pint please, John,' nothing more. And back he would go to his little group. They really kept themselves to themselves, as if they were trained to, like. Turns out they was SAS.

SHEP

One of the games the sergeants played was called Spoons. Worrit is, you get two blokes sitting opposite each other across a table and each of them puts a tablespoon in their mouths. The first bloke bows his head over the table and the other bloke tries to whack him on the back of the head with the spoon he's holding in his mouth. Then it's the other blokes turn. First one to give in. At least that's what they told us.

Dick was a steward, the clown of the ship. He had false teeth and wore the ring pulls from beer cans in his hair like dreadlock jewellery, you know. One of the sergeants asked him if he wanted a go and Dick being Dick jumped at it. So he puts this spoon in his mouth and the sergeant sat opposite him bows his head. Dick does his best and gives the soldier a knock on the head with the spoon.

'How d'yer like that!' Dick goes pleased with himself.

'Right, your turn,' the sergeant goes, so Dick puts his head down.

And as he does, unbeknownst to him, one of the sergeants standing around the table pulls out a massive ladle they've nicked from the galley and whacks Dick on the back of the head with it.

'Bloody hell!' Dick said as he came up reeling, 'How the fook did you do that?' The ladle's been hidden well of sight again by now, of course. 'Right, come here!' said Dick, determined to give his opponent as good as he got.

The sergeant bows his head, Dick tries to swing the spoon in his mouth down on this sergeant's head as hard as he can, but his false teeth are wobbling all over the place, so it's hardly a great whack.

Dick's turn to be whacked. And then he gets it with the ladle again. And again. And it goes on for some time until his head was starting to bleed at what point I had to say, 'Woh,' I says, 'perhaps we should call it a day there, eh? We've had a laff, we had some fun, but you're going to knock him out in a minute.'

BRIAN

I'm afraid it was a lot more formal for the officers. This note was slipped under my door the day after we left Portsmouth:

> The senior naval officer and officers of NP1850 request the pleasure of your company for drinks at 1900 on Tuesday 27th April.

Nevertheless we all got along well enough in our little snug bar when the booze was flowing. It was during our hours on watch that things weren't so pleasant at first.

JOHN

Most of the sergeants got to know me by name as it was only me and another barman, Pete Smith, working in the For'ard Lounge. If things was really busy we'd have a couple of squaddies helping out too now and then.

I remember having a laff with one corporal in the bar about our pay. How we was gerrin five hundred quid a week to be down here and they would be gerrin just a pound a day when they was out in the frigging trenches. And to make things worse for 'em they was used to paying 11p a pint for beer in their barracks, but now they had to pay North Sea Ferries prices. They was up in arms!

'Well, when I come back,' this corporal says to me, 'I'm going to come looking for you, John. And you can give me a bloody handout!'

FRANKIE

We served meals in the ship's main restaurant. It's big, it seats five hundred, but since we had nine hundred soldiers on board we had to have them in two sittings every meal time. They'd queue up at the servery and some of us would be there doling out bits and bobs for their tea. I'd always be nice as pie to them, give them a smile and a wink, make a joke, like:

'I tell you what, soldier, I'll swap you some of your bacon for my sausage.'

But it didn't always go down too well with these macho squaddies, you know.

WENDY

She's right. It didn't. So I don't know what came over me when a few days into the trip I decided to dress up in drag and play piano for the Toms in their bar. I thought they needed something to keep their morale up, you know't I mean? After all they was probably going to face battle down there in the Falklands soon and they might be a bunch of homophobic squaddies, but they was on our ship now and it was our job to look after 'em best we could. So I thought, being an entertainer, I should entertain them the only way I knew how. I purron an emerald green dress, shooshed up my hair, put on some dangly earrings and a bit of slap on my face. Some of us pushed and pulled the bleeding heavy piano I'd borrowed from Reverend Andrews out of the crew mess and into the Conti Bar. Well, there was hundreds of 'em in there. Hundreds of squaddies. And I thought to myself, 'You'll need a drink 'ere, darling, for your nerves.'

So I had a quick gin and tonic and I launched into a good old fashioned sing-along, you know't I mean? Well, worrit was, the paras was wary at first. Well, they would be, coz it was so different to what they were used to, wunt it. They looked at us like we'd come from a spaceship. I mean, talk about oil and water! But some of them had heard us having our fun nights in the crew mess and they wanted to know what all the fuss was about. So I belted out 'Old Faithful' and 'Red Red Robin', 'Knees up Mother Brown', 'It's a Long Way to Tipperary', and before long I had them eating out me hand. The whole place was singing along. They loved it. And any hecklers I just gave as good I got, like I did back in the St. Andrews Club in Hull. That seemed to do the trick.

JOHN

The Toms' bar was below the sergeants' where I was working and we could all hear the fun they was having as Wendy played, it was that loud. Some of the sergeants went down to see what all the fuss was about. Everyone loved it.

WENDY

When word got round about these nights with the Toms, the sergeants wanted a go too. So I played for them sometimes in their mess in the for'ard lounge and then even for the officers in the snug bar on the after end of the ship. So the piano was shifted from one end of the ship to the other. Not by me, I hasten to add! I think we got some strapping soldiers to do it or summat. But mainly I played it in the Continental Bar where the Toms had their mess. I'd decorate it in tinsel and Christmas decorations, even though it was the middle of bloody summer, coz it was the only stuff I could find on board, wunt it.

MALLY

There was four of us cooks doing nights. And we had to do all the baking, the bread work and the butchering for the following day. Doing all that for a thousand troops every day was a bit awkward so eventually 2 Para sent down some of their chefs to help out. We had a bread-making machine which broke down pretty quickly on the way south. I called up one of our engineers and asked him if he could fix it.

'Yeah,' he said sucking in the air like they do, 'but it'll take a month.'

'Well then the troops and the crew will have no bread coz there's no way we can keep up by hand,' I said.

The next night I came on for my shift and the bread machine was fixed. Funny that!

We cooked off some meats every night so it was ready for the next day. And one night we was doing this and one of our lads came into the galley and goes:

'There's a few of the paras lying on the deck outside here.'

'Well, they're probably drunk and collapsed out there, it's no bother,' I goes.

'No,' the lad goes, 'they've not collapsed, they was crawling along.'

'What do you mean crawling along?' I goes, so I went outside and saw these paras and I says, 'Worra yer doing?'

'Oh we just lost something. We're just looking for it,' this para says and then they all get up and leave.

By the time I get back in the galley the whole joints of lamb and beef I'd cooked had gone missing. The sods had nicked 'em. But they was hungry, see?

We couldn't give anyone extras if they came to the galley asking. From the Colonels down to the Toms we had to treat everybody the same. No matter who they was. Even our own crew what we'd worked with for years. If we didn't, we would have run out of food before we got half way to Ascension Island.

I had to say something after that night and they purra guard on the galley from then on.

FRANKIE

Just before we got to Freetown we heard about the sinking of the Argy ship the *Belgrano*. I was getting the bond ready to take to the officers in their lounge at the time, you know, the ciggies and the booze. There was loads of squaddies just outside the stores where I was stocking up my trolley from, just sitting around, playing cards, tekkin piss out of me, out of each other, the usual stuff. And then the news comes on over the tannoy that the *Belgrano* was sunk.

Well, the fooking cheer that went up among the paratroopers gave me chills so that I nearly dropped the bottles of scotch I was loading up. Somewhere down in the South Atlantic this ship had been blown up by one of our submarines and hundreds of men died because of it. Died from the explosions, or drowned in icy seas. And I got chills not just because of all those poor souls lost, but because of the way these soldiers around me was celebrating like a load of gorillas. And what was worse, it suddenly occurred to me, if that could happen to the Argy ships, what might happen to ours in return?

Well, two days later we found out, dint we?

BRIAN

Freetown, Sierra Leone – 3 May 1982

We made it to Freetown a week after leaving Portsmouth. When we got there myself and one of the third engineers – Derrick Frizzell, an Irishman too – went out on deck with some rods to have a wee go at fishing. This must have been just before the guard was put on the galley because we raided it to get bait for our lines. We nicked some slices of cooked ham and slices of bread and dumped them in a little pile on the deck at our feet, then when we needed some bait we stuck a piece on our hooks trying to catch some of these mega-sized tropical deep sea fish. There were even hammerhead sharks down there. It was night time, we'd all had a few drinks and a lot of the paras were milling about watching what we were up to, treading on the bait on the deck as they leaned over the side, but we paid no mind to that. It was only bait. After an hour with no bites we got fed up and decided we'd go back to the bar as it would be more interesting than fishing.

'Mind if I have that?' says one of the paras pointing at the by now manky trodden on ham and bread.

'What for?' Derrick says.

'For eating,' he goes.

'But look at the state of it! It's only good for bait.'

'Bait, my arse!' he says, picking up a handful of ham, stuffing it between a couple of gammy slices of bread and sticking it all in his mouth.

Hungry? They must have been bloody ravenous!

Being the radio operator, the lads knew I was the first to get all sorts of information. All orders came through the radio room in code, Morse code, and reading it was like magic to the rest of the crew. Of course modern satellite communications gear changed all that. We radio officers can send and receive Morse code at a rate of about thirty-two words a minute. An average word is classed as having five characters so that's about one hundred and sixty characters a minute. It's like a second language to us. Once learnt it's never forgotten. I can still do it now. The Radio Officer was the only officer who had to be fully qualified before he went to sea. I went to the Marine Radio and Radar College in Belfast for three years obtaining my first class ticket and radar maintenance ticket. Then I joined a ship under a senior R.O. for six months before I could take over my own station. You not only did the comms on board but looked after the bridge electronics (echo sounders, direction finder, steering gear, fire detection systems, radars and so forth). This made you quite useful because once the ship left port, say on a six-week run to Australia, you were the only contact with land and all the ships working business came through the radio office. Also a ship with no working radar isn't going anywhere in dense fog. So Radio officers on deep sea ships were the captain's best friends.

So when I told Derrick some girls who worked in the British Embassy in Freetown had radioed a coded message across to say they wanted to come aboard the ship for a drink he took my word as gospel, and he could barely contain himself. Well, it might have been all right for Wendy and Frankie and the like, being stuck on the ship for a week already and God knows how much longer with all these blokes, but for the rest of us it would be hard going at times, if you get me. There were only three women on board, remember. One was Carol, who was sixty-odd, one was Shirley who was with Bill, and one was Jeanie Woodcock, who was... well, Jeanie Woodcock.

So when I showed Derrick this signal I'd decoded and written out from Freetown, saying these girls were keen to come, he hurried off to prepare his cabin. He tidied up, spread a cloth over the table and bought every kind of drink you could imagine: Tia Maria, Drambuie, Cointreau, Malibu, all the popular drinks. He put some Disco tapes on the cassette player, you know. Caesar's Palace we were calling his cabin by the time he'd finished getting it ready, and loads of us blokes crowded in there and started drinking and having a grand time.

Ten o'clock comes and Derrick's wondering where the hell the women from the embassy are. 'I bought all this booze for them and they haven't even bloody arrived yet.'

'Oh, well,' I said with a twinkle in my eye, 'Never mind, we'll just have to drink it all instead.'

That's when the penny dropped. Steam was virtually shooting out of Derrick's ears when he realised we had faked those messages from the embassy in the radio room. There were never any girls coming. We just knew he'd lay on such a good spread for us if he thought they were. He saw the funny side pretty quickly, luckily, and we all had a grand time, as usual.

FRANKIE

Carol, who was one of only three women on the ship now and a good friend of mine, said she was leaving at Freetown.

Well, actually, she told me, she was 'advised' to go. She was older than most of us, you see, and they didn't think it was 'appropriate' to send a sixty-year-old lady down there. But we was only supposed to be taking the troops to Ascension Island then coming back anyway, so why wasn't it *appropriate*? That got me wondering.

Carol was gutted. In tears she was. And as she got off she said to me, 'Francis,' she always called me Francis, you see, 'Francis,' she says, 'Are you coming? I hear it's going to get bad. You should gerroff wimme.'

Carol and me we was good friends, even though I was only early twenties at the time. 'If you gerroff here,' she said trying to cheer herself up, 'we could go for a night out in Freetown before we go home. Think of all those lovely big black men!'

Well, I did… think about all those lovely big black men, I mean. So I went to see Captain.

'Captain Ellerby,' I says, 'I think I'm going to gerroff here and go back with Carol.'

'What on earth for?' Ellerby goes.

'Well, it's been nice up to now, we've had a laff, but if it's going to get dangerous, I'm no hero, that's for sure,' I said tugging nervously at me jewellery – I always wore lots of delicate gold chains round me neck at the time, you see.

'Look, Francis,' he used to call me Francis too, 'don't believe what anyone tells you or what you hear on the radio, everything will be fine.'

'Are you sure?' I goes.

'It'll be *fine*,' he says.

So I goes back to Carol and says, 'I think I better stay Carol, I can't leave her, can I?' I said referring to *Norland*.

Well, Carol wasn't too happy. 'They'll be trouble down there, I bet you a thousand pounds to a piece of shit there will.'

'But Captain Ellerby said it'll be fine, love,' I goes and I left it at that.

Well, I lived to regret that, dint I?

DAVE

As we left Freetown the senior naval officer from the *Europic* ferry came over the radio and gave us the course we were going to steer down to Ascension Island. I happened to be on watch at the time so he told me we were required to go out to the fairway buoy and then steer a circular course, so not A to B in a straight line, but in a curve which is a bit ridiculous because you only generally do that if you're going east to west, you don't do it if you're going south. So I said, 'Well, we're not doing that. We're going to go out to the fairway buoy, due east till we hit the longitude of Ascension Island and then turning ninety degrees and go straight down.'

'Well, why?' this navy officer snapped at me.

'Three reasons,' I said, 'First, if they fly helicopters up to us for any reason it's easier to find us because we're on that longitude. Second, there are Russian trawlers about so it will keep them guessing. And third, we've got a commander on board and you're only a lieutenant-commander, so we outrank you.'

Besides it was much easier to sail that way, so I did.

There was a bit of an upbeat air among the soldiers on board after the *Belgrano* was sunk so when it came to crossing the equator a couple of days later they were very much up for getting involved in our sailors' ritual of Crossing the Line, which is a tradition that has been going on forever. It was a kind of initiation rite for sailors that have never crossed over the equator before. It certainly happened to me when I first joined the Merchant Navy at the age of sixteen as a deck apprentice. It used to be brutal back then, but things had lightened up a bit by '82. Sailors who have already crossed the equator are called Shellbacks or Sons of Neptune and those who hadn't are called Pollywogs. There's a kind of mock court presided over by King Neptune, who one of us would dress up as, in a terrible paper crown and George Cross costume wielding a floppy paper trident, with another bloke as his missus Amphitrite, in a wig and dress.

WENDY

No that wasn't me, in case, you was wondering! Don't matter what they say, these macho ones, given half a chance they'd all be in a dress and a wig, you know't I mean?

DAVE

We told the soldiers about it the night before and they were keen. We told them it was a ceremony for crossing the imaginary line around the middle of the earth, which is actually marked by little red lights all along the equator out at sea and if they looked out now on the starboard side they would see one of them.

'Really? Oh yeah!' they went, 'That's amazing!'

Of course it was only the side light on *Europic* ferry they were looking at, silly sods!

But, as I say, years ago it could be brutal with the Pollywogs having hot sauce, aftershave and whole uncooked eggs put in their mouths. During the ceremony, the Pollywogs had to go through a number of increasingly embarrassing ordeals: wearing clothing inside out and backwards; getting shaved; walking the plank; crawling on hands and knees on non-skid coated decks; being swatted with short lengths of fire hose; being locked in stocks and pillories and pelted with mushy fruit; being locked in a water coffin of salt-water; crawling through chutes or large tubs of rotting rubbish; kissing the belly of some fat bloke playing the Royal Baby, which was coated with axle grease and hair clippings; all for the entertainment of the Shellbacks of course. But in '82 it was more like everyone just getting on deck in nothing but their shorts…

FRANKIE

Heaven!

DAVE

…and the Pollywogs having grease from the engine room smeared all over them, flour chucked over their heads, then they'd be thrown into the swimming pool, which since it was 85 degrees that day, was quite a welcome feeling for them. But by the end everyone was covered in shit and dunked in the pool, Pollywog or Shellback. It passed the time and kept everyone in good spirits.

FRANKIE

Until we heard HMS *Sheffield* was destroyed by an Argy missile. It was one of our ships. One of the first to reach the South Atlantic, long before we even made it to Ascension Island.

There was no more cheering, no more fun or celebrating then. All I saw as I pushed my trolley full of bond through the corridors lined with soldiers was a load of frightened little boys. Me included.

3

A SLIGHT
CHANGE OF PLAN

FRANKIE

I have to admit I was dead jealous of Wendy. I was stuck up on A deck pandering to all the officers in their little boring snug bar on the arse end of the ship. It was exhausting. Officers' stewards had to work longer hours than the other crew members and all I heard about was Wendy and the others four decks down living it up with all those hunky squaddies. We didn't even have any decent music on the radio. When I wanted to listen to a bit of Soft Cell or Human League we had to have the fooking World Service on all the time to see if Mrs Thatcher had come to some agreement with the Argies. Although, I have to say, even I was listening in, saying to myself, 'Come on Maggie, get something sorted so we can all turn round and go home before we have any more *Belgrano*s or *Sheffield*s, you know. But the cow didn't get it sorted, did she?'

It wasn't just me up there, by the way. There were four of

us officers' stewards all together, including Martin, or Mimi as she called herself. She lives in Oswaldtwistle these days. Lovely person. *Lovely person* and a good worker too, even though she was a touchy poof.

WENDY

Well, I nearly lost me rag with you lot, dint I?

FRANKIE

Nearly?!

WENDY

Well, worrit was, *some people* didn't appreciate was how hard I worked too. Playing the piano and entertaining the troops every bleeding night was not a breeze. It was hard work. And I did all that after I'd finished my shifts as a steward. I was bleeding knackered every morning.

FRANKIE

I bet you were!

There were some perks to being stuck up on A deck though. Sometimes the troops would have to be doing their fitness training up top and they'd have to run laps of A deck then jump down to the deck below just behind the bridge and do a lap of that deck too. Well, where they had to jump down was just outside the officers' pantry where I kept all the stores for 'em and I remember calling to Mimi, 'Come and look at this, love!' and we both had our noses pressed up against the glass of the pantry window as the boys jumped past it in their little shorts. Oo, it was like a waterfall of bollocks. Lovely!

SHEP

Some of 2 Para was mad bastards. And the closer we got to the Falklands the more excited some of 'em got.

'See him over there?' one of the sergeants said to me one day, pointing to one of the Toms on deck, 'That's Trev. He'll be frothing at the mouth by the time we get to the South Atlantic. He can't wait. We were all in a line-up once at the barracks. Princess Royal was visiting and there she was working her way down the ranks and I'm thinking please don't stop at Trev, please don't stop at Trev. And what does she do? She stops at Trev and asks: "So what made you join the army, soldier?" A standard question, you know, to which you're supposed to give the stock answer "To serve queen and country, ma'am." But Trev answers, "Because I like killing people, ma'am."'

MALLY

Between midnight and three in morning was our time for going down to the shipping containers and bringing up the supplies we needed. So we'd look at this map what had been drawn up of all the containers and we'd go and find the meat or worrever it was we was looking for that night. So this one night we was looking for eggs and we found them in one of the containers at the back, but there was also this crate of beer in there un'all.

'What's this beer doing in here?' I says to one of the other lads. And he says, 'Dunno.'

So I says, 'Look at the map again and make sure there's only meant to be eggs in here, will yer?'

So he did and it was right, there shurrav only been eggs in there. Beer was in another container altogether.

'Well, if there's only meant to be eggs in here nobody's going to miss this crate of beer then, are they, if we borryit.'

So we did.

SHEP

The Royal Navy sparkies needed a room big enough to put all the communications equipment in so they'd knocked two cabins through into one and in the process cracked one of the windows. It was my job to replace it. So as I'm doing the job I'm looking in through the hole where the new window is going to be, looking in on all this incredible equipment. I mean, there was even a bloody red phone, hotline to Maggie. It was jaw-dropping. And the sparkies saw me gawping and said, 'I hope you're not a Russian spy!'

'No, I'm not,' I goes, 'I'd have no idea what any of this kit does anyway.'

'Well, I'll show you,' one of these sparkies goes. And then he says, 'Think of a country!'

'India,' I says.

'Think of a town!'

'Calcutta.'

'Who do you want to ring in Calcutta?' he says.

'I don't know,' I goes, 'I don't know anybody in bleeding Calcutta.'

'All right,' the sparkie goes, 'How about the Post Master?'

I shrugged as the bloke tapped a few buttons and held the phone up to my ear. After a few seconds I heard this Indian accent going, 'Central Post Office, Calcutta, how can I help?'

'Fook me,' I goes, 'that's a smart bit of kit tharr is.'

And you gorra remember that this was only 1982. None of your smart phones then.

'You never saw any of this, Shep, OK?' the sparky winked.

'Yeah you're all right,' I said picking up me drill and getting on with me work.

I kept that drill in sight all the time in those days. Ever since the time it went walkabout, remember?

KEITH

Oh aye. Long before *Norland* was requisitioned, a passenger came to me complaining about not being able to sleep in her cabin because of all the light coming in through the wall. Well, this didn't sound right so I went with Shep along to her cabin and sure enough when we turned the lights off there was all these thin beams of lights slicing through the darkness. Very weird. So we traced these beams to their source. And we realised that the light was coming through from the next door cabin because someone had taken all the screws out from the bulkhead, so there was these little holes everywhere. Well, it didn't take us long to work out that these holes was being used as spy holes for a peeping Tom, like. And there was only one person who would do something like that.

SHEP

Pervy.

KEITH

Yeah. 'Pervy'. He was in his late thirties then. Tall, skinny with a great big bush of grey hair on his head, always a bit shifty, like. He was well known for having a stack of girlie mags in his locker so large that had we slung them overboard the ship would have risen six feet out of the water. He was bound to be the culprit.

SHEP

So I burst into his cabin and used my keys to open his locker. And underneath the copies of *Knave* and *Men Only* was only my bloody electric drill! The dirty bastard.

WENDY

Well, I have to thank Pervy really. Those holes came in useful when 2 Para was on board. I could sit there all day peeping through to the cabin next door and watch the soldiers taking a shower. Oo, happy as a sandboy, I was! They was never short of towels down there. I was always on hand, if you know't I mean! And now I'd started to bond with the squaddies through my piano playing, I had to admit I was having the time of my life. I feel terrible saying it really, but we was transporting these boys off to a war and I thought I was at bleeding Butlins, I did!

FRANKIE

Yeah, well they thought they was at Butlins un'all and she was the bouncy castle.

BOB

Ascension Island – 7 May 1982

Although 2 Para were beginning to bond with our crew there were certain tensions, I have to admit, between us officers and the navy party on board, as Brian alluded to earlier. For me it was interesting, let's say, as I was the one chief officer to two captains now, so to speak: the navy commander Chris Esplin-Jones and our captain, Don Ellerby. Chris had three lieutenant-commanders under him. One for aviation, one for communications and one for the flight decks. They had engineers on board to run the reverse osmosis machine (to turn sea water into fresh water) as we didn't have the manpower for that, so there were about twenty-eight in the navy party all in all. The navy petty officers were strutting about the ship, taking over, ticking things off lists without even discussing it with Lloyd the chief engineer or myself and we were quick to tell them that wasn't the way it worked on this ship.

To be fair to them, that generation of navy officers were on a learning curve as much as we were. It was all new to them, as they had never been mixed up with the Merchant Navy in the way that officers serving in the Second World War had to be. The Merchant Navy and Royal Navy are two different cultures completely. Nevertheless, they had chartered the ship from us, you see, so they were supposed to be merely the liaison between us and the navy fleet, but they were receiving orders from the fleet command and actioning them without communicating with us first, so it seemed as if they were trying to take over. Consequently the tension grew and it wasn't long before we were told formally that we were now officially under navy command and if we didn't do what we were told we could be court martialled under the Navy Discipline Act. We were all made to sign the Official Secrets Act and it was then that I had the feeling the navy had other plans for the *Norland* than just being a transporter ship.

It was all getting a bit too fractious as we sailed south, we really needed to get our act together, work together, and I felt the commanders were being particularly unfair to our captain Don Ellerby, so without Don's knowledge, Lloyd the chief engineer and I had a discussion with the senior naval officer during which I said:

'Chris, look, we are all in the same boat here and if this is going to work we need to sit down and we have to have some kind of agreement. So let's draw up a document that details exactly who has what responsibility, proper standing orders signed by both parties then we all know where we stand and we can all move forward.'

'And what if I don't agree to this?' Chris asked, perhaps guessing our response already, which was basically to threaten him.

'You need to agree to this,' Lloyd said, 'We know the ship. You don't. Without our co-operation, this ship is going nowhere.'

Chris paused for what seemed like a very long moment and then said, 'Can I have twenty-four hours to think about it?'

'OK,' Lloyd and I agreed.

The following day the entire naval party were walking around the ship with notebooks asking everyone in our crew about their jobs and how everything worked, so Chris was clearly preparing for a mutiny, as it were, thinking about the naval party having a go at running the ship themselves. But perhaps in the end it seemed too overwhelming for them, and Chris knew really that it was absurd to suggest he was able to override Don on certain matters, so he came back to us at five o'clock that evening and through gritted teeth said, 'All right.'

And that was when we produced a document called the *Norland*'s War Orders, detailing the distribution of responsibilities. Things went a lot more smoothly from then on. Everyone knew what they were doing and no one was stepping on anyone else's toes.

Then, at Ascension Island the entire crew was assembled in the Continental Bar, which had now become the privates' bar, and we were informed in a meeting with the commanders of the Task Force that, as I had suspected, there had been a slight change of plan.

FRANKIE

Slight change of plan? Slight is how my arse looked in my favourite pale blue kecks. This was not a *slight* change of plan! I knew something was up in Freetown, when we stopped there and they chucked Carol off – I mean, 'advised' her to leave.

BOB

Chris Esplin-Jones informed everyone that it had been decided that the *Norland* was now needed to take the troops all the way into the Falklands and form part of the amphibious landing party along with HMS *Fearless* and HMS *Intrepid*, two warships also carrying troops into the battle zone.

This wasn't quite what we signed up for so the crew were all given the opportunity for the last time to disembark at Ascension Island and fly back to England.

None of us did. We all stayed. We had no intention of leaving the ship or our crew mates, despite the terrible news of the *Belgrano* and the *Sheffield*. Besides we were told we would ferry the troops into San Carlos Water behind *Fearless* and *Intrepid*, then, when the men had gone ashore on their small landing crafts, we would turnabout and anchor far outside the battle zone. Little did we know that this plan was also going to change for the worse, as far as we were concerned, by the time we arrived at the Falkland Islands.

BRIAN

For me and the wife, Liz, we had been through all this before in the Far East. We had met in Malaysia when I had flown to Singapore in 1964 to join Shell Eastern's fleet as they had just won a huge contract to supply American and South Vietnamese forces with fuel for the war, mainly aviation fuel (JP4) but also gas for automobiles. I spent from 1965 to1974 on tankers running up to Saigon, Nha Trang, Danang and so forth returning to Singapore each time to load up again. At that time Liz and I lived in Johor Baharu in Malaysia, just across the causeway from Singapore so I was able to see her and the kids each time I was back from Vietnam. We were on double wages and paid no tax, but it was quite dangerous and still quite nerve-racking for her. My ship was mined in Nha Trang and hit with rocket-propelled grenades just south of Saigon. The bridge and radio room were sandbagged up and we wore protective clothing but the main danger was from the cargo exploding. JP4 was a very volatile fuel that the British wouldn't touch but the Americans used it in their Phantoms and Skyhawks. Luckily we came out of all that unscathed and, although Liz was obviously not over the moon when I called her to say I was going further south now in the Atlantic, it was not the first time either of us had the experience of me going into a war zone. And surely this couldn't be as bad as the Vietnam War, could it now?

KEITH

When they told us we was going all the way into Falklands, everyone was up for it. Then they told us that we could write a letter home before we sailed that evening and make one call each to home at the RAF base in Georgetown on Ascension. After that, as we moved off towards the Falklands, we'd be in a communications blackout for strategic reasons. *Norland* had anchored in the bay outside Georgetown so a Sea King Helicopter had to shuttle us back and forth to the island in groups of ten (that's as many as it could handle, you see).

I called my wife Jayne. She'd had no problem with me coming

down to Ascension, but when I told her about going into the Falklands itself she was in bits, you know. It was hard enough seeing her and my two girls on the quayside back in Hull waving me goodbye, waving their little Union Jacks with the paratroopers' band playing *Land of Hope and Glory* as we edged away. And then I only thought we'd be gone for a few weeks. But suddenly, as I'm trying to have a decent conversation down this new-fangled satellite phone, with its bad echo and having to remember to press the button every time before I speak otherwise Jayne misses what I've said, it felt like there was a chance we wouldn't be coming back.

JOHN

Especially when they handed us them ID cards what said:

> If you are captured you are required under the provisions of Article 17 of the Prisoner of War Convention 1949, to give your captors the information set out overleaf so that your capture may be reported to your next-of-kin.
>
> When you are interrogated, but not before, tear off the duplicate portion and give it to the interrogator. GIVE NO OTHER INFORMATION. Once this card has been issued to you you must carry it upon you at all times. In your own interest you must ensure that the particulars of your rank are kept up to date.

KEITH

And especially when Esplin-Jones said to everyone, 'One more thing you'll be required to do before we set off south, is to write a will.'

4

FROM TEA AND BUNS TO SUBMACHINE GUNS

WENDY

Ascension Island is slap bang in the middle of the Atlantic, just south of the equator. It was so nice to be there. Not just because we made it one piece, but because it was mafting. Really hot. Which meant there was paratroopers all over the place with their tops off, you know 't I mean?

Worrit was, we was all given the option to fly home from here now that the *Norland* had been ordered to carry the paratroopers all the way into the Falklands. But none of us took them up on the offer. I, for one, was too busy watching those muscly torsos sizzling in the sun.

Unfortunately two of the para lads fell asleep on some deckchairs aft and got themselves severely sunburnt. Their sore skin would have been punishment enough, bless 'em, but then the RSM found out (the Regimental Sergeant Major, that is). His name was Malcolm Simpson. He was tall and handsome and hard as bloody nails. A proper bastard, I thought, at first.

'Where do you think you are?' he bellowed at these poor sunburnt soldiers, 'Does this look like the Costa Del bleeding Sol?'

'No, sir,' they winced.

'This is not a bloody holiday, so get your uniforms and full bergens on now and meet me on the car deck in five minutes!'

Well, he had them running laps of the car deck for ages with their thick uniforms and heavy back packs rubbing on that burnt skin of theirs. Can you imagine?

DAVE

As an apprentice in navigation you are always taught not to get too close to other ships, show your lights bright at night and keep clear communication with other vessels. Now we were in a total blackout at night, on a darkened bridge, using night sights from sniper rifles through which we could just about see the grey shape of another ship. Bin liners were stuck over the windows all over the rest of the ship. It was pretty rudimentary stuff.

BOB

Is that why you lost the task force, Dave?

DAVE

I did not lose the task force, thank you, Bob! What actually happened was, after the *Europic* ferry caught up with us, we both joined up with the *Canberra* and the *Elk* (the former and latter were two more merchant ferries) as well as two major naval assault ships, an RFA ship (Royal Fleet Auxiliary) and the merchant ship

Atlantic Conveyor, which had been converted to carry aircraft. We rendezvoused on 10 May a thousand miles to the north-west of the island of Tristan de Cunha. We were only a couple of thousand miles from the Falklands by now, but there were Russian trawlers about, Russian aircraft flew over at one point, there was even a report of a submarine periscope. It was 1982 remember, the Cold War and all that. So we started sailing in World War Two style convoys, a mass of ships all different angles and distances off the guide ship, all zig-zagging at the same time on a given signal. This was to confuse the Russians, you see.

But the communications were not coming through for some reason. I had a Royal Navy signalman on the bridge who was supposed to tell me what was going on, but he didn't seem to know what he was doing, useless bugger! I knew something was up when the *Atlantic Conveyor* came across our bow, far too close! It was five or six in the morning, just before breaking light.

'They've altered course, obviously,' I said to myself after recovering from the shock of that close shave, 'And so I clearly haven't received the signal to do the same. But I can see where they are now the dawn is breaking so I'll leave it a little bit then alter course and slip back into the convoy, as if nothing happened.' Which I would have gotten away with if Don, the captain, hadn't have woken just then. He came up to the bridge, blinking through sleepy eyes. He must have thought he was still dreaming when he went, 'Dave, where's the rest of the task force?'

KEITH

It must have been around the same time when some of us was down below on the car deck, working our way through the maze of shipping containers, trying to assess what supplies we had left and where they was, when someone shouted 'Fire! Fire!'

There was smoke coming out of the laundry room, which was also on the car deck. So we all hurried over and tackled the fire, which thankfully had not got out of hand yet. Then before we knew it, instead of a 'Thank you, lads,' all the *Norland* crew was up in front of Commander Esplin-Jones and he's giving us a doing for trying to sabotage the mission.

'We have no idea which one of you is responsible for this reckless act,' he said, 'But when we find out, the repercussions will be severe. People could have been killed. And if you think something like this is going to get you home any quicker you've got another think coming.'

WENDY

As if it was one of us! We'd never do anything to harm our ship. The *Norland* was ours, not theirs, not the Royal Navy's, you know't I mean? Someone was hoping a fire would cause us to turn round and head home, but I could guarantee it was not one of us. As for who it really was, though, we still had no idea.

BOB

That little episode with the fire didn't do our already tense relationship with the navy party any good. But at least relations between us and 2 Para were going from strength to strength. Even if they did try and scam us on occasions.

Steve Hughes was a clever bloke, one of the 2 Para doctors. One of the reasons that 2 Para got off relatively lightly during the war and that so many injured soldiers survived was the training he gave them on the way down. For example, he made every single one of them learn how to put an intravenous drip in so they could do it in the battlefield if necessary. To do this training properly they needed some fresh meat to train on, but where would they find these live guinea pigs, I wonder?

Well, because the *Norland* crew had been contracted into the military by signing the Naval Discipline Act we were then issued with those Prisoner of War ID cards, as John mentioned. Now, on the other side to the bit that talks about what to do if captured, there's space for personal details, name, date of birth, height, weight, religion, eye colour and blood group. But none of us knew our blood groups. So 'in order to find out' we all had to go up to the ship's medical room and have a sample taken. It was, however, only when we got there that we realised the sample was going to be taken by a very nervous soldier being trained to put in these drips, who proceeded to poke around in your arm with a needle, both soldier and crew member almost fainting, until he managed to find a vein.

Then it was Dereck Begg's turn. Beggy was a third engineer. Very thin, intelligent, very dry sense of humour, steam train enthusiast, you know the type. He held out his pasty skinny arm and the soldier doing him poked about for ages before he gave up, but with encouragement from the army medic doing the training, he tried again on Beggy's other arm. The soldier, almost breaking down after repeated fruitless attempts, at last managed to find a vein and draw a syringe full of blood which he held up like a trophy, elated, and to which Beggy says:

'Fooking hell, that's torn it. I was saving that for an erection.'

SHEP

It was when we was getting closer to the Falklands that the entire Task Force came together. The ships that had headed for South

Georgia way before us; all the warships like HMS *Hermes*, HMS *Invincible*, HMS *Fearless* and HMS *Intrepid*; the frigates like HMS *Plymouth* and *Andromeda*. Probably thirty or forty ships there, plus all the tankers and RFA supply ships, then ships like the *Norland*, Merchant Navy vessels that had been converted, the *Canberra* and the *QE2*, the list goes on and on and on. I thought I'd seen some things in my time. My father – a sailor all his life – had sailed on the great Russian convoys; I'd seen a flotilla or two myself, burr I had never been part of something like this. It was an armada. There's no other word for it. I was standing on the helicopter deck one day looking out behind us and there was ships as far as the eye could see. I know some might say, 'Yeah right, on yer bike, daft lad,' but I was there and we was part of an armada, Francis Drake-like, inexorably steaming through the waves on our way to war.

JOHN

Five days before frigging D-Day, the day we was meant to land the troops in San Carlos Water, they stopped the soldiers drinking booze. No more booze allowed, so I was left serving teas and coffees. The troops had to get fit and focused, you see. And everything suddenly got a lot more serious.

I was having a cup of coffee myself in the crew mess one morning, just waking myself up, you know. I was sitting by the window, a round porthole, still half asleep, when this Harrier Jump Jet descends into view from nowhere and hovers outside the window. I look out. He's so close I can see the pilot, and he sees me and salutes. I'm frozen, like, with me cup of coffee half way to my mouth, my jaw on the frigging floor, you know. So I find myself saluting back and up he goes out of sight again. If it had been whiskey I'd been drinking I might have thought I'd had a bit too much, but it wasn't my imagination. I s'pose we was well and truly in the battle zone now.

BOB

Travelling all that way from Portsmouth to Freetown, Freetown to Ascension, and then from Ascension to the Falklands (three weeks since leaving Portsmouth) with a thousand personnel on board, we were producing a lot more waste than we could handle. So at the end of each day the soldiers would take black bin liners full of rubbish and toss it off the back of the ship. There was nowhere else for it to go unfortunately but into the sea. However, we had to disperse it so that the full black bags didn't act like a trail of bread crumbs giving away our position in the ocean. The best way to do this, we found, was to shoot the bags from the deck at the stern of the ship and thereby give the troops some firing practice at the same time. After Ascension Island the army offered us – the officers, the crew, all of us – a chance to have some shooting practice at this trail of rubbish too.

WENDY

I had no intention of getting one of those Paras' weapons in my hands. Well, not the kind that fires bullets anyway, you know't mean?

FRANKIE

Me neither. When they came asking me to have a go I said to 'em, 'Do I look like fooking Annie Oakley?'

WENDY

But Jeanie, Jeanie Woodcock, she was well up for it. Jeanie and I was very good friends. Ah, Jeanie she was such a darling. She was only in her thirties then. Only a little thing, plump, God love her, but she had such a great big personality. She would bowl into any room, no matter where, and whoever was in there would know she'd arrived, you know't I mean? She loved Barbra Streisand and I loved Barbra Streisand, so we had a lot in common we did.

She showed me a picture once, of a beautiful young girl and she goes, 'Who's that? Bet you can't guess who tharr is!'

'Not a clue,' I said. I really didn't have the foggiest.

'It's me, int it,' she smiled.

'Give over!' I goes.

'It is!' she said.

And when she said that I looked a bit closer and I realised it *was* her, un'all. I'd always known her with a kind of slightly deformed face, you see. Coz she'd had this terrible car accident years before I first met her and she had to spend weeks in hospital with a fractured skull, broken jaw and badly injured legs.

FRANKIE

She had these awful, ill-fitting dentures too because of the injuries, you know, and when she used to sing – coz she used to love Barbra Streisand just as much as Wendy did and, even though she had a terrible voice, she'd sing 'People', you know from *Funny Girl*, at the top of her lungs – and these dentures used to fly across the room. But she didn't care. It was actually a joy to see someone like that. Someone so confident. Well, I guess you could go one of two ways after such a trauma as she had. Inwards or outwards. She definitely went outwards. And we all loved her for it.

MALLY

She used to like a Bacardi did Jeanie. Always a double-double she'd ask for. So when they told her we was under rationing when the troops came on board she said, 'Well, I'll just have a small treble then.'

KEITH

I was on the deck aft having a go with one of the rifles, supervised by the soldiers, like. Then Jeanie arrives and they offer her one too.

She turns her nose up at it and points to one of the submachine guns on the table.

'Worr about one of them?' she says.

The soldiers loved Jeanie's style and quite happily put the machine gun in her hands, not worrying that she'd never so much as held a water pistol in her life.

So she aimed at the black bin bags bobbing around in the wake of the ship and fired. The kickback was so great for little Jeanie she was suddenly dancing around all over deck and the gun was pointing every way but at the water, so a couple of Paras had to jump on her and tear her paralysed finger from the trigger before we all got shot to bits.

SHEP

One of the army sergeants asked me to take my deck crew buddies out to the arse end of the ship every evening after tea for shooting practice.

45s: hand guns. SLRs: rifles what could knock a brick wall down at a thousand metres. SMGs: submachine guns and the like. The soldiers would shoot. We would shoot. We had a little competition to make it interesting. See who could shoot the most. Guess who won? We did. The soldiers was not used to aiming at something while the ground beneath their feet pitched and rolled; while the targets bobbed up and down in the waves. Us able seamen being used to the undulation of the sea had much more success hitting our targets than the trained soldiers did.

I didn't think at the time though why we was even there shooting guns off the stern every night. I thought it was just a game, just about building camaraderie between them and us, you know.

But the commanders had other ideas.

WENDY

Some of the bloody squaddies was using the seagulls as targets during their firing practice. Then, worrit was, one of them killed an albatross and so there was hell on. The merchant seamen went crackers coz it's a very bad omen to kill an albatross as far as sailors are concerned. Even Captain Ellerby got on the tannoy and warned any other soldiers against doing anything like it again. I mean, as if we needed summat like that at a time like this, you know't I mean?

BOB

Norland officers were often invited to briefings along with the navy and army commanders, which now included Colonel H. Jones, Commanding Officer of 2 Para, who'd just parachuted in, under cover of night, on to the ferry as we approached the Falklands, all very James Bond-like. In one such meeting the Colonel was going on about how concerned he was that the ship was very visible from the air because of its big orange funnel.

Norland was a big ship with a black hull and white superstructure and, yes, an orange funnel on the top. It was quite distinctive. However, I told him that in my opinion the funnel was irrelevant as the white superstructure was even more visible and the pilot of an aircraft would easily see us anyway. H. Jones became quite paranoid about it and asked that I get the crew to paint it black. This was not possible whilst the ship was at sea with the engines running as we did not have access to the top of the funnel. But Colonel H. would not let the matter rest so in the end we gave him some bamboo poles, rollers and black paint and told him to get his soldiers to paint it if he insisted it was done. He took up the challenge and some of 2 Para were tasked to do the job. Unfortunately the poles were not long enough so we ended up with an orange stripe on the top of the funnel and, as there was a lot of wind on the top deck, some very paint spattered paras!

KEITH

In another of those briefings we had been told that once the troops had gone ashore in their landing vessels, instead of then manoeuvring out of the battle zone, as we had been told back in Ascension, we would up anchor and move closer to the beachheads behind HMS *Fearless* and HMS *Intrepid*, which obviously didn't go down too well. And now in another meeting Colonel Jones was telling us something different again.

'The order has changed,' he said in his suave public school accent, '*Norland* will be going first, then *Fearless*, then *Intrepid*.'

FRANKIE

When Keith told me that I thought, 'Don't sound very fearless or intrepid to me!'

KEITH

The Colonel continued, 'Should the *Norland* be hit I am advising you to ram the ship into the beach.'

'And what about my crew?' Captain Ellerby said, looking paler every minute.

'Well, they have had some arms training now…'

I thought, you mean shooting bin bags off the arse end of the ship while Jeanie Woodcock nearly kills us all with a machine gun?

'…so we would advise them to grab a firearm and run ashore concealing themselves,' he cleared his throat, 'in the trees.'

The next morning I was stood on deck as the sun rose over the Falklands giving me my first glimpse of them barren islands, famous, as it turns out, for not having a single bloody tree growing there!

5

SHHH!

FRANKIE

Falklands Sound – 20 May 1982. 2300HRS

The for'ard lounge was full of squaddies. All in their proper battle gear, great big heavy backpacks. All of them putting on their camouflage face paint, from those thick black sticks. Some of 'em was keeping up the usual macho bravado, you know, but others was scared. It was obvious, but they just couldn't admit it, not in front of their army mates.

JOHN

And frigging Frankie waltzes in there and says, 'Right, who wants help with their eyeliner? Come on, I'm a dab hand at make-up, I'll give yer hand.'

It just helped to break the tension a bit, you know.

FRANKIE

That's not to say I wasn't terrified meself. I was. It was a moonless night, specially chosen I daresay to keep us from being spotted. Black bin liners stuck all over the port holes. Very hi-tech, I thought! And we're gliding into the sound when John Dent, one of the third engineers comes over to me and says, ''Ere, Francis, take these' he says, 'There might be some noise going on in a hour or so,' and he handed me a pair of them ear muff things what they use in the engine room, bless him. What a gent! He was built like a brick shithouse was our John, but he was a gentle giant, you know, and I'll never forget what a lovely gesture that was. But that's how we all looked after each other on *Norland*, you see?

KEITH

Falklands Sound - 21 May 1982 0200HRS
We was all meant to be on our bunks in *defence positions*, as they called it, by then. We had been told that should we hit a mine whilst we was standing, the sheer force of the vibrations through the ship (even if we was nowhere near the impact site) would break every bone in our bodies. So the safest place to be was lying on our bunks with our life jackets on keeping out the road.

But I knew these boys from 2 Para were due to get in the landing craft and basically go into battle between 03:45 and 04:15 in the morning with nothing more inside them than a cup of tea and a cold sandwich. I just couldn't let them go like that. So it's 02:00 in morning and me and the cooks are whipping up bacon and egg rolls in the galley and some of the stewards are serving them to the troops. Then RSM Simpson came steaming in ranting, 'You and your men need to stand down now, that's an order!'

And I said, 'I'm sorry, Mal, but I can't let those men go off to war without something hot inside them.'

WENDY

Oo, I could give 'em something hot inside 'em!

KEITH

And all the crew are standing behind me now facing down this Regimental Sergeant Major. 'The quicker we can get this food down them and say a proper goodbye,' I went on, 'the sooner we can get to our defence positions, all right?'

He was fuming, but perhaps he understood the bond that had been forming between us and the 2 Para boys, despite everything, so he did a swift about turn and buggered off, leaving us to serve the hot rolls.

MALLY

They was all kitted up, blacked up, ready for going and crowded in the for'ard lounge as the egg and bacon butties was handed out. As I peered in to see how my cooking was going down I was disappointed at first to see that a few of 'em weren't eating at all. But that was understandable I s'pose, since they must have been nervous. I bloody well wurrav been. But plenty of others was making the most of the last decent meal they was likely to get for some time. If someone left their food coz they couldn't eat, out of nerves or worrever, another soldier would grab it and have two lots.

KEITH

I went up to Captain Ellerby a bit later and told him about that run in with RSM Simpson. I said, 'Captain, I'm really sorry, but I'm afraid I disobeyed an order.'

I told him what I'd done and he just goes, 'You're a civilian, Keith. You're not in the armed forces and I'm your boss, so the RSM can go…whistle.'

SHEP

0330HRS

Deathly silence as we glide into Falkland Sound in the heart of the Falklands under cover of darkness. Total blackout, no one is to make a sound, not a peep that might give away our position as we try to offload the troops without the Argies getting wind of it.

Ellerby, Esplin-Jones and Bob are on the bridge communicating via walkie-talkie with us on the bow where the anchor chains are.

'OK, Shep,' Ellerby's voice comes softly from my handset, 'Drop anchor.'

'Right you are, Captain.'

And me and Dave go about releasing the anchor chains.

Nothing.

What is it, Shep?' comes Ellerby's voice.

'It's the bloody chains,' I hiss into walkie-talkie, 'It's been such a long journey they've gone and rusted up.'

BOB

We'd reached the anchorage point. This whole thing, all those ships behind us, our movements had been planned with precision down to the second. It was indeed beautiful timing. Like Horse Guards' parade. That's how it worked. I had to pass through point alpha and point x-ray at the designated time. If I didn't it would mess it up for all those other ships behind us. We had to drop anchor now. And we had to do all this in absolute silence.

SHEP

The only way was to use a hammer to loosen the chains so the anchor would fall. I told the Captain this and he gave me the go ahead. So I lifted up me hammer, took a deep breath and—

WHACK!

BOB

Suddenly the silence was broken by a massive clank of metal on metal. Again and again as they tried to loosen the chains. Every clank ringing out through the silence was eerie enough without the thought that each one might be alerting the Argentinians to our position.

SHEP

Eventually the chains loosened, thank God.

BOB

But now the silence was shredded by the sound of the anchor chains endlessly unravelling as the anchor fell into what apparently was a bottomless sea beneath us. Up on the bridge we were wincing with every noise, until at last it stopped and silence thankfully reigned again.

JOHN

0345HRS

Down on the car deck the shell doors was open and the first two landing craft was there waiting to fill up with men and ammunition.

It's a huge drop to sea level from the open doors, coz they usually open out onto the dockside so cars can roll on and off; it wasn't cut out for loading men onto frigging LCUs. So the soldiers had to wait for the swell of the tide to bring the boats up higher, nearer to the open shell doors and then jump down. You can see how this was just waiting to go frigging pear-shaped and one lad actually broke his leg as he jumped and had to be hauled out again, never making it to the fighting. Lucky for him, some might say!

There was a chain gang of troops and crew quietly passing equipment into the boats and Wendy in middle of them all. It was frigging hilarious when the RSM, who was used to being the one doing the ordering, was getting ordered about by Wendy going:

'Hurry up, hurry up! The boys need their ammo, darling. Come on!'

KEITH

And then, just as the anchor chains had, the silence was shattered again by the tannoy going:

BING BONG!

And Captain Ellerby's voice came through it going, 'I'd just like to take this opportunity to wish our troops well on their mission. We do all hope you all come back safely. Good luck.'

BING BONG!

The army and navy officers went white.

And it was many years later when I returned to the Falklands, for the thirtieth anniversary in fact, and got talking to a farmer from Goose Green, that he told me he was up at that early hour on 21 May back in '82 making a cup of tea in his kitchen when he heard this mysterious sound coming out of the night.

BING BONG!

'Did you hear that?' he said to his wife, who nodded back, mouth open, like.

If it reached them all the way in Goose Green, it was a wonder the Argentinians didn't trace it back to us.

Just before he jumped in one of the landing craft himself, Colonel H. Jones came up to me and said, 'I have to admit, Keith, I had my doubts, but my troops are fit and well thanks to you. Mission accomplished.' He saluted me and off he went into the night. I was as proud as a peacock.

So now the boats are fully loaded with 2 Para and they set off to battle. It was sad to see them go and they was sad to be leaving us too. We all waved to each other and, just in case we hadn't done enough to give the game away, Wendy starts waving his white handkerchief about and crying, 'Bye, boys, bye now!'

SHEP

'Someone shurrim up!' I goes, 'And grab that white hanky he's flapping about before the Argies see it and think we're surrendering.

FRANKIE

Bill, the union man, married to Shirley one of the stewardesses, had said to me on the way down, 'Now, Francis, don't get too close to any of these soldiers,' and he didn't even mean in a sexual way, just as friends, you know, 'Don't get too friendly with any of these army boys, coz when they all come back you'll be looking for 'em and they might not have made it, and then you'll be in a right state.'

Well, it was really sinking in what he meant now, wunt it.

WENDY

It was so sad to see them go. The carnival atmosphere of the first few weeks had gone. You could see it on the lads' faces. They knew they was going off to war now. It was really happening. I had stopped playing the piano at night a good few days ago now. It just didn't seem right anymore. But the squaddies was still trying to make jokes and that though, right up to the last minute as the last ones was getting in the boats.

Dave Brown he was one of the paras, God love him, and, worrit was, it was his twenty-first birthday that day. He was just twenty-one on 21 May 1982, the day we put them into the boats. Can you imagine? All his squaddie mates laughed about it and joked that to honour his special day there would no doubt be a fly-by by the Argentinian air force.

Unfortunately they was bloody right. There was.

6

LCU, NGS, Y2K AND G&T

BOB

San Carlos Water, Falklands – 21 May 1982. 0430HRS

I was responsible for piloting the *Norland* into the anchorage in San Carlos Water in the dead of night, after the landing craft full of troops had left us. As we silently steamed in I finally broached the subject with the senior naval officer, Esplin-Jones, who was on the bridge with me.

'Chris,' I asked, 'So how come we are now the lead ship going into the bay, and not *Fearless* or *Intrepid*?'

He shuffled uncomfortably for a long moment before muttering, 'Well, Bob, to be honest, we're not sure if the entrance to the bay is mined or not.'

As you can imagine, I wasn't happy to hear that, but you couldn't deny it was good military thinking. Now the troops were all off, *Norland*, a mere passenger ferry, was expendable, whereas *Fearless* and *Intrepid*, both warships, were not.

But I didn't have much time to think about that then as the night was suddenly filled with red tracer bullets and the noise of enormous shells going off either side of us.

WENDY

My legs went like jelly.

FRANKIE

So did your fooking belly, darling.

WENDY

Twat!

BOB

Although we feel like we are now, at the time we were definitely not military men. Although myself, Don Ellerby, Keith and the other *Norland* officers had been to those briefings on the way down to the Falklands, some of the abbreviations and military jargon they used went right over our heads. In the notes it had actually stated that as soon as the LCUs had headed for the beaches, NGS would commence. Now I knew that LCU stood for Landing Craft Utility, but unfortunately, none of us had thought to question what the hell NGS stood for. Then, as the silence was obliterated by the immense noise of navy frigates, a mere four hundred yards either side of us, firing shells from their four-and-a-half-inch guns over the top of us into the hills, our crew were running about like headless chickens thinking we were under attack. But the navy liaison and the marines were all as cool as anything since they knew that NGS stood for Navy Gunfire Support.

I couldn't say I was scared, but all that noise and chaos on the first day was quite disturbing. I was just glad I had to be up on the bridge and could see what was going on. Whereas everyone else was ordered to go to their bunks, which for many of the *Norland* crew was right down on G deck, five flights of stairs below the water line. I was buggered if I was going down there at a time like this. We had all seen plenty of war movies on the big screen before then, but suddenly now it felt like we were on the big screen ourselves.

WENDY

We all had our own cabins on *Norland*, but when there was an air raid threat we all had to go down to G deck, right at the bottom of the ship, and double up in cabins. And if there was a submarine threat then we all had to rush up to the top decks and double up there instead. I shared with Jeanie. I was on top bunk, she was on bottom. And on that first night we was down in G deck and I says to her, 'If I don't see you in morning, love,' I goes, 'I'll see you in heaven.'

And although she was as terrified as me, I think she replied with summat like, 'You in heaven? Give over!'

KEITH

The shelling and the gunfire died down after a few hours and then we was left with a ghost ship. We was all sitting around and we didn't know what to do with ourselves. For the past few weeks the *Norland* had been alive with a thousand troops and we had been working day and night to look after them all as best we could. And suddenly they had all gone, except for a few marines that remained to look after us, and the small navy crew. It was the weirdest thing. No matter what a pain in the arse they had been at first, no matter how much tension there had been with all these different officers trying to tell us what to do, we missed them all.

BOB

We missed their weapons too. You see, since our role had changed from troopship to landing ship back in Ascension we had insisted that the ship be armed appropriately to protect her and us. So machine guns had been set up on the bridge wings and on the upper decks, with even missile launchers and all sorts up there. But when the time came for the troops to go ashore we soon realised they had buggered off with all the good gear! And this was cause for great concern to me when at about ten o'clock in the morning, the Argentinians began their air raids.

WENDY

That klaxon went off and it was all down to G deck in emergency positions again. Those Argy jet fighters screaming overhead and bombs dropping all over the place. The anchor chains would rattle with the vibrations from the bombs hitting the water and send the most eerie sounds through the lower decks where we had to be. And worrit it was, some of them raids lasted for six hours at a time.

FRANKIE

Oo, that bloody klaxon! That made me worse that thing. It was horrendous. Now, if it had been a small little *ding dong*, you know, like Avon calling, that would have been fine by me, but no, it had to be that horrible moan of the klaxon, dint it?

DAVE

The klaxon we used for air raids was an old Norwegian foghorn, a hand-driven thing that we had had on the bridge for years, just in case all else mechanical failed and we had nothing to sound our presence in low visibility. But we had never had to use it before so it had just stood on the bridge gathering dust. In fact some of us used to use its horn as an ash tray as it stood at just the right height when you were sitting there on watch. So by the time it came to actually use it for the first time to signal the air raids one of the other second mates pushed down on the handle and a cloud of ash spewed from it so big we thought the bridge had been hit.

KEITH

As an officer I was stationed on one of the upper decks during the air raids. And it was on one of those first raids, as the tannoy went, 'Air raid warning red, air raid warning red!' and I was sat there waiting for the bombs to start dropping again, that I heard someone singing: 'Land of hope and glory, mother of the free…'

And Jeanie Woodcock comes round the corner with her life-jacket on, a Para's helmet, which was far too big for her head, waving a little Union Jack.

I said, 'Jeanie, you've got to take cover, lass.'

'Look 'ere,' she goes, 'It's fooking ninety steps down to G deck and ninety fooking steps back up again. I can't be arsed to do it even once, let alone if this goes on time after time all day!'

'But it's emergency positions, love, that's what the klaxon means. You've got to go down to your emergency position.'

Well, she showed me with her fingers just what she thought of emergency positions and carried on doing endless circuits of the foyer and restaurant, waving her flag and singing as the bombs dropped all around us.

FRANKIE

And what about Bill and Shirley! That was one of the saddest things I've ever seen in my life. As I'm running downstairs I see stewardess Shirley sitting in a chair in the restaurant in tears and her husband Bill, the union man, knelt in front of her holding her hands and singing *Loverboy* to her or some other such tune, you know.

I said, 'Bill, Shirley we've got to get below.'

Bill said, 'We're not going anywhere. We're staying up here on D deck.'

'If we're going to die,' Shirley sniffed, 'We're going to die together, like this.'

And Bill carried on holding her hands and singing to her as I did a runner down below. I'm not eloquent enough to say how deeply touching that scene was to me. I mean, they had sailed together for years. What a way to end their sea careers, I thought. It really was fitting for them to go like that. They both liked their Bacardis, both of them, but right then they was dead sober. It was nothing to do with the drink. They knew exactly what they was doing.

And it dawned on me then, if they thought they was going to die, that this could be it for me too. I was fooking terrified. And they was right to do what they did. I'd have been better off up there too. It was so claustrophobic down there, hearing all these terrible sounds and not knowing where they was coming from. And if we had been sunk, being right down there below the water line, we would have been the first to gerrit.

SHEP

I wasn't going down there neither. I sat down on a chair on C deck right near the doors. Someone had to be around to keep an eye on the ship. Someone had to look after her. And that was my job, as far as I was concerned. So when they came round telling me to get out road and onto me bunk I told 'em where to stick it.

DAVE

Me too. I went down there once, but I never did it again. I stayed on the bridge for all subsequent air raids. But on one of my first watches up there, waiting for the next raid, I saw these shapes coming over the hills ahead of us, on a heading just off our starboard bow.

'Bandits at one o'clock!' I shouted. Not sure why I put it like that exactly, but everyone on the bridge laughed at me, not so much because of my dramatic terminology, but because what I'd actually spotted was a flock of geese.

BRIAN

I have to say, I thought to myself, as I'm lying on a bunk down in G deck, 'This is just going to be a graveyard if anything hits.'

BOB

Some people felt safer down there hidden out of sight, and at the end of the day if there was any shrapnel flying at the side of the ship you would be better off below the waterline, but if there had been a fire or a flood you were certainly more vulnerable.

James Draper was second engineer. A bit of a conspiracy theorist was our Jim, the kind of bloke that would stock up his cupboards for Y2K. For the voyage to the Falklands he came on board at Hull with his own NATO tin helmet, a personal emergency light and some webbing which he kept his emergency Mars Bars in. We all used to laugh at him but he was actually well equipped if something ever did go wrong. Much better than the rest of us. He used to inspect all the lifeboats personally. He was the man who was going to survive if the shit ever hit the fan. During air raids he would don his tin helmet and webbing then go into the pantry in the kitchen, fill the sink with water and hide underneath it, stacking up empty beer barrels all around himself. It was quite a sight.

JOHN

After a few air raids lying on my bunk I said to my mate Pete Samsan, 'All that action going on up there and we're missing it all. Let's go up and have a look. I can't stand it stuck down here not knowing where all those frigging bangs and crashes are coming from.'

So me and Pete went up and aft, out on deck on the arse end of the ship and as soon as we got out there I looked up and all I could see was the grey belly of this Argentine Skyhawk fighter plane roaring over me head, filling the sky, it was that low. Well, I shit meself, as did Pete who threw himself back onto the floor. Except I was behind him so he landed right on top of me and there we was in a heap on deck with these great jets of water exploding up around *Norland* as the bombs hit the sea.

BOB

It wasn't just the Argentinian planes that were terrifying us. Our own Harrier jets would often pass the ship so low and fast that everything inside would shake.

FRANKIE

I popped my head up on deck once too. Well, as I say, it was too claustrophobic for me down there on G deck. But only once, mind, did I do that. As soon as I heard one of them bangs up close I screamed and ran back down below squealing to Wendy, 'Captain said we'd be safe. Safe my arse!'

'Well, of course he said that,' Wendy goes as we're both running to our emergency stations as best you can on trembling legs, 'He didn't want you to leave ship, did he, because you wash and iron his shirts for him, you daft cow.'

Oo, the cheeky sod, I thought, I was just his bleeding Widow Twankey, wasn't I? That's why he was so keen for me to stay.

Being a poofter un'all I had no qualms about screaming me tits off and running about like a headless chicken when I was frightened. And in a way that meant I was better off than the straight crew members who felt like they needed to put on a brave face. You see, I would say, 'I'm fooking scared stiff,' if I was. But most of the others had a butch image to uphold and they'd have to bottle it all up if they were scared.

JOHN

Anybody who said they weren't frightened when them frigging bombs were going off are lying gits.

FRANKIE

I saw one of the crew on the arse end of the ship one day sat there, terrified, quaking in his boots, like, physically shaking. So I goes to him, 'What's the matter with you?'

And he goes, 'Oh, I'm all right, I've just got DTs or summat.'

He was so frightened, but he couldn't say. He couldn't say

because it wasn't the done thing if you was a straight bloke, especially back in them days. And so in the end I think I might have come out of it all less disturbed than some coz I was getting it all off my chest from the off.

BOB

It was on day one, whilst ships were continuing to offload gear and troops in Falklands Sound that the destroyer *Antrim* was hit by a thousand-pound bomb, which luckily did not explode; but the frigate *Ardent* was not so lucky. About four in the afternoon a lone Skyhawk dropped two bombs which straddled *Ardent*, both failing to explode. *Ardent* proceeded west as ordered and about an hour later three planes swooped in and dropped three bombs on her. Two of the bombs exploded in the hangar area sending their Sea Cat rocket launcher flying up into the air before it crashed down onto the flight deck. A Lynx helicopter was destroyed too, whilst the third bomb, although it did not explode, crashed through the aft auxiliary machinery room. Six o'clock and another wave of attacks saw more bombs exploding aft, penetrating the ship or exploding in the water flooding the hull. Twenty-two men, I believe, lost their lives before the ship sunk the following morning. It was sobering news and suddenly the possible fate of *Norland* was staring us in the face.

BRIAN

Whenever I was on watch and I looked out and saw those Skyhawks roaring overhead and dropping bombs all around us it got me thinking back to being in Vietnam. You see, after the end of the Vietnam War the Americans sold off quite a number of their Skyhawks to Argentina. They were very useful bombers and fighter planes because they could take off from small airfields and carriers. I often wondered, whilst under attack in San Carlos, if any of those aircraft were the actual ones I had helped to fuel in Vietnam a decade earlier. They most probably were.

FRANKIE

One morning I was there with me trolley getting the officers bond, coz they was all drunks. Except Bob, of course.

BOB

Thank you, Frankie!

FRANKIE

No, seriously, I was there outside the duty free shop where I'd just got all their booze and cigarettes from and I bumped into her, into Wendy, on the shopping concourse and she goes:

'Oo, nice quiet day today, lass, eh?'

And no sooner had she said it than that bloody klaxon goes.

I said, 'You big mouthed cow,' and I cleared off, ran for it, screaming like Old Mother Riley down to my cabin, emergency positions, leaving all the bond on the trolley standing in the middle of road.

'Course, when I got back after the air raid it was all gone. Marines, navy or some of our crew, God knows who, had nicked it all.

I would have been better off with the squaddies onshore. I could have dug a nice big hole for meself and stayed there till it was all over. Instead of being trapped on a ship with nowhere to run to.

But funnily enough Commander Hughes, one of the navy officers, one that looked like Christopher Biggins, very camp, I'm not saying he was gay, it's just the way he looked, he was a lovely man and he said to me one day, 'Francis,' he said, 'Francis, I think you're really brave.'

Well, he couldn't have been talking to me, could he, so I said, 'You what? I don't think I heard you right.'

He said, 'I think you're brave.'

So I goes, 'Worrever made you think that?'

'Well,' he goes, 'you're always the first to get straight back to work after an air raid.'

'Oh,' I says as the penny drops, 'That's not coz I'm brave, that's coz I've got so much to do. I've got Captain's bed to make, chief engineer's room to do, I've got so many chores on I'll never gerrem done by the end of my shift if I don't get straight back to work, especially now there's more officers than ever on board what with you navy lot too!'

BOB

Our designated anchorage in San Carlos was very close in to the land under the shadow of a hill. We were there, as per usual, a few nights in. It was a stormy night, weather-wise. But things had cleared a little by the next morning, so visibility was fine for the two Skyhawks that came screaming over the hill releasing their bombs at their target.

Their target, it seems, was the *Norland* in its anchorage.

I'm convinced that that was the first day of a change of plan for the Argentinians. They had decided not to leave us, the transport ships, alone any longer; it was time to hit us too.

And they hit their target dead on.

7

READ ALL ABOUT IT! MERCHANT SHIP SUNK IN FALKLANDS

BOB

The bombers' target was indeed the *Norland* in its anchorage. The thing was, we weren't in the anchorage anymore; we were not exactly where they had spotted us the day before, thanks to that bad weather during the night.

When the weather had blown up, the ship had dragged her anchor, as she was wont to do being relatively light. So we all had to turn to, we got the engines started and the bow thrusters on and we re-anchored the ship, but now it was just three or four hundred yards away from where it had been at sunset. Those bombs hit the water exactly where the *Norland* had been parked the previous day. And if we had still been there our fate would have been the same as the *Ardent*'s, if not worse.

KEITH

But the funny thing was, as the days wore on, after air raid upon air raid, you started to get used to it. We even got blasé about it. I was sitting one day in the duty free shop with one of the shop assistants and we was trying out the aftershave testers as if we was in bloody Boots in Hull on a Saturday afternoon, even though two five-hundred-pound bombs was hitting the water four hundred yards away. And there was Jeanie in her helmet and lifejacket, still marching round the deck, singing and waving her flag. And Bill and Shirley singing golden oldies in the restaurant. For three or four days, five air raids a day, sometimes up to six hours, these unreal air raids went on.

But then things got very real again when the *Antelope* was sunk.

BOB

San Carlos Water – 23 May 1982

HMS *Antelope* was one of those navy frigates supplying the NGS, protecting the beachhead as our troops secured it in the first days. But it was a few days in when she came under attack from four Argentine Skyhawks. She had been our escort that day and she was currently north of us steaming down our port side. I was on the bridge when the jets came in through the entrance to the sound very low. One of them got right astern of her, going very fast and as the pilot pulled the stick back to gain altitude he dropped this thousand-pound bomb, which I saw make a little black hole in her starboard side, but it didn't explode. And as the jet tried to clear the ship it hit the radar scanner on the top of the mast, peeled off and disappeared over the hills.

DAVE

I was out in the lifeboat at the time taking an injured marine to HMS *Fearless*. As the bombs started dropping we had to hurtle into the back of her, as you could drive straight into *Fearless*, her being a warship properly equipped to receive landing craft, unlike *Norland*. We waited it out there. It was terrifying though. I wasn't really happy being inside a warship. I mean, they were the targets after all. I felt we would have been safer out in the open water, believe it or not. But it was all over very quickly. The raid, I mean, but not the consequences.

BOB

Unfortunately, we later found out that that bomb killed one crew member as it pierced the ship. The *Antelope* managed to hit one of the other jets with its 20mm cannon and the Skyhawk crashed through the *Antelope's* main mast killing its pilot and showering us with shrapnel, we were that close. But not before the pilot had put another bomb in the *Antelope's* hull. This bomb, like the first, did not explode. The ship proceeded to more sheltered waters so that two bomb disposal experts could come aboard and attempt to diffuse the bombs. Unfortunately, their efforts resulted in one of the bombs detonating and ripping the ship apart, killing one of the bomb disposal team and severely injuring the other. Major fires started all over the ship then, so the order was given to abandon her and, five minutes after the last person (the Captain) had left her on 24 May, the *Antelope's* missile magazines began exploding.

WENDY

Oo, those explosions was like some awful fireworks display, lighting up the night sky and everyone and everything around in the bay, including us on *Norland*. If the Argies had taken the opportunity then to have us they could have, there was no cover from darkness that night.

Thankfully they didn't, but the order was given to send all the survivors from HMS *Antelope* to *Norland*. So we had to convert one of our lounges into a medical room pretty quick and although we had medics on board we all pitched in to help the wounded, you know't I mean?

KEITH

The *Antelope* seemed to be only a few hundred yards away from us as it exploded. I had never seen anything like it in my life. Never seen a ship actually melt. I watched the main mast curl up like a withering flower and then she split in two, right down the midships.

Most of the survivors that arrived on *Norland* were OK. I mean, they was in shock with just a bit of trouble from smoke inhalation and that. But most of them came aboard in nothing but their underwear coz it was the middle of the night and some hadn't had chance to grab any clothes, which just wasn't right, especially in the middle of winter which it was down in the South Atlantic in May and June. So we had a whip-round, like. Everyone dug deep in their own suitcases to donate a piece of clothing and we piled them all into this big wooden crate on one of the car decks and then all the survivors could come and chose a set of clothes.

Now all the survivors – *Antelope* being a navy frigate in the '80s – was all men, so Frankie, being Frankie, found a lady's bra, God knows where (perhaps Carol had left some stuff behind when she went) and he hid this bra among the pile of clothes, so when one of the men came to choose his clothes he pulled out this bra.

FRANKIE

Well, it was important to have a laff, even at a time like that. And I think it did the survivors as much good as it did us to keep smiling, you know.

JOHN

Talking of having a laff, remember Dick? He was a steward, the one that got his head bashed in playing frigging Spoons, and we was chatting with a couple of the cooks near the galley one day, Frankie, me and Dick and suddenly we hear this faint noise, almost like a gong, you know, boom! And I see Frankie's eyes start going and his feet start twitching.

'You hear that?' he goes.

'What?' Dick goes.

'That fooking sound.'

Boom! It goes again. It was still quite faint at this point but a little louder this time.

'I can't hear nowt, can you?' Dick goes to the rest of us.

'Well, now you come to mention it, Frankie,' I goes, coz I definitely heard it that time.

And then it came again, louder this time, a definite BOOM and it echoed round the galley, vibrating through the bulkheads.

'Sounds like bombs underwater or summat. Getting closer,' Dick went.

'There's been no air raid warning,' I goes.

'It's not coming from the air by the sound of it, it's coming from a submarine or summat,' Dick goes, looking worried himself now, although he was still leaning against the wall like it was just another afternoon in the park or summat.

'Oo, I don't fooking care if there's been a warning or not, I'm not sticking around to find out,' Frankie goes and he starts darting out the room looking as if to go down to emergency positions.'

'Well, you can't go down below, Frankie,' Dick goes, 'It's coming from underwater, int it.'

BOOM!

'Fooking hell!' Frankie goes, scampering back into the galley looking for a place to hide.

BOOM! BOOM!

'What we going to do?' he squeals.

These booms was coming faster and louder than ever now, and Dick is still leaning against the wall like nothing's happening and even me and the cooks are about to run for it.

Until I notice Dick pissing himself laughing.

Frankie's got his head in a saucepan and he's hiding in the pantry by now. And I look down at Dick's foot where he's leaning against the wall and I can see that each boom is coming from his foot kicking against the bulkhead, the bleeding sod.

BOB
Falklands Sound — 25 May 1982
After four or five days of air raids we sailed out of San Carlos Water and rendezvoused with the *Canberra*, which was anchored offshore, outside the sound, in the Transport and Logistics zone, which was out of range of the Skyhawks.

FRANKIE

I wish we was anchored in the fooking Transport and Logistics zone instead of being in the thick of it when all the bother was happening.

BOB

Well, the *Canberra* was an enormous ship and bright white too. It wouldn't have stood a chance in San Carlos Water.

WENDY

If it wasn't for the angels what was watching over us those past few days neither would we, you know't I mean?

BOB

So both *Canberra* and *Norland* sailed together to meet the *QE2* which had brought the 7th Gurkha Rifles and the 16th Field Ambulance down to South Georgia.

KEITH

We had no escort for the day or so it took us to get to South Georgia so it was quite worrying. And we thought the conditions was bad enough in the Falklands, but it was proper Antarctic conditions in South Georgia. A hundred knot gales and if you touched the railings on deck your hand would have stuck to it.

BRIAN

Without any escort it did feel a wee bit isolated out there, then at three o'clock in the afternoon I picked up a distress message from a British BP tanker called the *British Wye*. They said there was a Hercules making passes over them and the crew were pushing bombs out of the back of the plane. We thought we were out of range from all the Skyhawks and what not out in these waters because the Argentinians, as we understood it, had no long-range bombers. But they had decided to use a Hercules, which is essentially a transport plane, for carrying troops and cargo over long distances, which enabled them to reach all that way into the South Atlantic Ocean and they were literally chucking bombs out by hand, you see. Some of them actually hit the *British Wye*, but bounced off the forecastle, at which point they sent a distress signal out on 500 kHz and luckily we happened to be near enough to receive it and pass it on to the Task Force. So much for being out of the battle zone!

WENDY

We saw a couple of whales on the way down, these enormous black calloused heads breaking through the surface, staring at us ridiculous humans, you know't I mean, wondering no doubt what we was doing disturbing their peace and bombing their seas all over a bit of barren land, a God forsaken place on the arse end of the world. And worrit was, the waters was black too down there, as black as Whitby jet.

KEITH

As we approached land and anchored in Grytviken harbour there was mountains everywhere with these incredible blue glaciers cutting through them. Tugboats and trawlers helped ferry the people between ships. We transferred the *Antelope* survivors onto the *QE2* and took on the Gurkhas and Field Ambulance. About a month before, the marines had kicked out the handful of Argentinians what had occupied South Georgia and they'd formed a garrison there, you see, so it was pretty quiet now.

MALLY
Bloody right it was quiet, thank God. Doing nights in the galley us cooks would sleep in the daytime, but since the air raids always happened during the day, we wasn't getting no sleep. In the end we gave up trying and was existing on no sleep at all. When we set off to South Georgia it was bliss for a bit. We slept like logs.

KEITH
After the Falklands the snug bar on the aft end of the ship, what was the officers' mess during the war, was renamed the Antelope Bar.

MV *Norland*
At Grytviken

27 May 1982

Dear Captain Ellerby,
This is a difficult letter to write, since you have been so good to we *Antelope*s that a few lines in thanks seem inadequate.

Nonetheless it has to be said that our passage in *Norland* has been exceptional; from the moment of arrival, despondently clutching our pitiful belongings, you raised our spirits with helping hands and a very warm welcome. The welcome did not stop there – throughout our short stay we have been overwhelmed by the friendliness and generosity of your entire ship's company and of NP1850, whose response to the very real needs of my people has been marvellous. You gave us clothes, hot meals, cool beer and even a party led most ably by Wendy. Your greatest act of generosity is the collection that your ship's company has spontaneously arranged for us: you may rest assured that it will be put to good use and from the bottom of our salty hearts we thank you for it.

  Again many thanks from all *Antelope*s to both *Norland* and NP1850; we will all cherish fond memories of our stay.

Yours,

Nick Tobin

Captain, HMS *Antelope*

JOHN

Having the Gurkhas on board was very different to having 2 Para. I mean, these little blokes from Nepal were psyched up to fight, but they was right out of their comfort zone out on the ocean. Their element is rough terrain and high altitudes, they have a reputation for being fierce fighters but as I passed by the shopping area they was all sitting on the seats there hugging each other and feeling seasick. If they got up they would be wobbling all over the place. One came up to me in the bar looking right queasy and barked:

'Drink!'

He looked like some of us did after a night on the piss so I poured him a large tomato juice with heaps of Tabasco sauce. A Bloody Mary minus the vodka coz they wasn't allowed alcohol. That seemed to sort him out.

KEITH

When we first came to serve them dinner they was pointing at the beef and we, trying to respect their culture, said, 'No beef,' what with them being Hindu and that.

'Yes beef,' they said.

'No,' we said thinking they didn't understand and that they thought it was some other meat.

'Yes!'

'No,' we said offering them some chicken instead.

'Yes beef!'

'No beef!'

'Yes beef!'

'No!'

MALLY

I s'pose the message didn't get through from the galley. We was told by the Gurkhas commanding officers that they had been given special permission to eat beef whilst they were on a war footing. They would even come into the galley and cook their own food sometimes. They had a funny way of cooking rice. Without water. It took bloody ages, but it tasted perfect. And they did a nice curry too. They let us have a taste. They were well-mannered lads on the whole.

JOHN

When they got used to the motion of the ship I saw them doing a little dance with their knives, these special curved knives they all have. They really know how to handle a frigging knife, I can tell you. Having them on board to look after was a nice change from being bombed in San Carlos.

KEITH

But as we arrived back in the Falklands to land them we saw the terrible sight of the *Atlantic Conveyor*, burnt out and sinking.

BOB

Atlantic Conveyor was a fifteen thousand-tonne roll-on/roll-off container ship owned by Cunard. Like us, before we successfully argued for weapons back in Ascension, she was not fitted with any defence system. She was requisitioned by the MOD to carry supplies and followed us down from Ascension Island. She was carrying all manner of artillery as well as Chinook helicopters, the new Sea Harriers and older Harrier jump jets.

On 25 May she was hit by two Exocet missiles fired by two Argentine jet fighters. They both hit her in the port side and, because of all the ammunition and fuel on board, she went up in flames. It was uncontrollable, nothing was saved from the ship and twelve men lost their lives.

KEITH

But then a little six-hundred-odd tonne merchant tug boat called the *Irishman*, what had also been requisitioned from Hull, was ordered to tow the burnt-out hull of the *Conveyor* all around the ocean as a decoy. There was three of these tugs in the area. The *Salvageman*, the *Irishman* and the *Yorkshireman*.

JOHN

Sounds like the beginning of a frigging joke, dunt it?

KEITH

Aye, but you wouldn't be laughing if you was among this poor handful of men on board the *Irishman*, towing this dirty great shell of a ship around the ocean so the Argies might think it was still in operation. Luckily they didn't fall for it. Lucky for the poor blokes on the *Irishman*, I mean, and eventually the *Conveyor* sunk three days later in the early morning of the 28th.

HMS *Coventry* was sunk that day too. Nineteen men on board lost their lives. It was tragic, but to be fair she was a destroyer, she was a warship, like HMS *Sheffield*, she was meant to be engaged in battle and unfortunately she was likely to be fired upon. So when the news reached us it was sad, but perhaps not surprising.

But these merchant tugs, they were not battle-ready. Like us. They all came from Hull, them three tugs. In fact Hull sent the most ships from one port to the Falklands: the three tugs, five trawlers and the *Norland*.

BOB

The South Atlantic is hostile enough even without a war going on. The enormous waves, the severe winds, blizzards, dense fog and hundreds of drifting icebergs some literally miles long. So for all those ships suffering battle damage the prospects were not good, unless there was immediate help. This help came in the form of tugs which could tow them to calmer areas where they could be repaired. United Towing Limited of Hull had only three tugs left by 1982 and had to send all of them down to the Falklands. *Salvageman* is bigger than the rest at around one and half thousand tonnes, but all three are highly manoeuvrable carrying portable salvage pumps, generators, air compressors, water cannon and so forth. The *Irishman* and *Yorkshireman* were instrumental in salvaging many damaged and wrecked ships in the task force.

BRIAN

As an Irishman, I'd never even heard of Hull and Yorkshire in my life until I was on the oil tanker called *Hatasia* back in the sixties, on which the quartermasters one day were fighting with each other about which way to turn the bloody wheel. One saying hard port the other saying hard to starboard until we ran aground off the coast of Sumatra. We were aground for a week and we were full of oil so they had to send another Japanese tanker down from Singapore to take the load from us. I was sitting on watch in the radio room and by this time all our power was running down, we were down to our last emergency batteries, when on channel 16 VHF comes this alien voice:

'*Ah-tazia! Ah-tazia!* This is *Yorkshireman*.'

Well, I hardly knew what he said at first, his Yorkshire accent was so new to me. But they came and pulled us out and when I went on board her I was amazed at all the gear they had on there. They went all over the world sorting out ships and rigs. She was just on her way back home after towing a rig to Japan when she got the call to come and get us out of trouble in Sumatra. Priceless wee ships they are.

JOHN

But back home in Hull in '82 the information was coming through that a Merchant Navy ship had been hit by missiles and sunk. The first Merchant Navy ship what was sunk in a war since World War Two. That was the *Atlantic Conveyor*.

KEITH

Michael Booth was a great guy. He was the North Sea Ferries personnel manager and liaison for the crew's families back in Hull. What with being a family man himself he understood what our wives and that might be going through so he really worked hard to get as much information from the MOD as possible and relay it to the families that all had a hotline number for Mike. The news was coming through that this Merchant Navy ship had been hit, but that was all Mike could get out of the MOD at first.

JOHN

So all our families was going spare, wunt they? The *Norland* was a Merchant Navy ship too and for all they knew back at home it was us what gorrit.

BRIAN

It had to be much worse for our wives than it was for us, even though we were in the thick of it. We didn't have time to worry and we knew what was going on from minute to minute. But our loved ones back home didn't have enough information: if you were safe, if you were in danger, even. Knowing something was better than knowing nothing as that got their imaginations working overtime. They heard a bulletin on the BBC every evening giving a list of ships hit and so forth. One evening they announced a British merchant ship had been hit and that there were casualties, but they didn't name it. They got into hot water over that I think, because you can imagine what it was like for the people listening back home.

KEITH

It was a good few agonising days for our wives and parents back in Hull before Mike managed to get the facts out of the MOD that it was the *Atlantic Conveyor* and not the *Norland* what gorrit.

JOHN

That was quite a low point, wunt it? Back in San Carlos, back getting bombed all day, the *Atlantic Conveyor* burnt out and sunk and then news that Colonel H. Jones, the commanding officer of our 2 Para boys had been killed un'all.

SHEP

Well, that was because he was so bloody gung-ho, wunt it? Me and some of the lads had a little bet on for how long it would take him to get killed. You knew it was only a matter of time, because he thought he was so clever to lead from the front.

JOHN

I think it was more that he was a really lovely bloke who cared about his troops and wouldn't ask them to do anything he wouldn't do himself. It was sad when he gorrit coz, what with him being a commanding officer, we all knew him by name. It was harder to know many of the troops by name coz there was so frigging many of them.

BOB

I agree with John. He was a great guy, much admired by his troops. The attack on Goose Green might have failed if it wasn't for H and his adjutant David Wood, who were both killed leading the offensive.

MALLY

We was running out of supplies by this time, so we was having to get by on basic rations. It was a real low point all round.

KEITH

The culprit behind the fire in the laundry room finally cracked too and owned up. Turns out it was one of the navy lads on board what was so scared about going to war he set this fire, hoping the ship would be so damaged it would have to turn back and we'd all go home before we even got to the Falklands.

SHEP

So much for the navy thinking they was our bosses! I saw this navy kid gerrin dragged away by a couple of marines to the arse end of the ship and we never saw him again.

KEITH

A couple of days later and we was landing the Gurkhas in San Carlos just as we had 2 Para nearly two long weeks before. We was dab hands now. Wendy was still there ordering the officers about, and then the landing craft was gone and once more the ship was a ghost ship. We was left there twiddling our thumbs and just waiting for the next bombs to drop.

FRANKIE

The next fooking bomb to drop was the news that we was now a POW ship and on our way to load up with Argies! Well, it was one thing picking up our troops and dropping them in the battle zone, but it was a whole other thing to pick up the enemy, wunt it?

8

THE
PRISON SHIP

BOB

We were given the order, the day after landing the Gurkhas, that we were to pick up five hundred Argentine prisoners from Goose Green. Prisoners-of-war captured by the British troops. And then we were to wait offshore with the *Hermes* group for further orders.

WENDY

I was frightened at first to have a load of Argies on board. Well, you would be, wunt yer? They wasn't exactly going to be happy to be there, you know't I mean? We watched as the marines escorted them on board and I remember being shocked and going, 'They're just little kids!'

JOHN

Coz they was all conscripts, you see. Not like our lot. Most of them had no choice. That Galtieri, president of Argentina at the time, he needed a lot of troops quickly, so apparently he trawled the schools and colleges, clubs and bars, wherever he could get hold of fit young men. Half of them had no idea how to fight, let alone what they was fighting for.

SHEP

That was why so many lives were lost on the *Belgrano*, in my opinion. Half of the crew was conscripts and had no idea what they was doing. If it had been us lot on that ship we would have known exactly how to evacuate safely. We was all trained, you see. It's what we do. It's what we know.

BOB

I don't think so. The lives were lost on *Belgrano* because she was torpedoed in deep water with no rescue services available. It was a ship from the Second World War with limited damage stability. It was nothing to do with conscripts or training.

KEITH

Anyway, most of the poor buggers was terrified to be on *Norland* especially as the marines shoved eight of them at a time into cabins that was only meant to sleep two and locked them in. But those that were traumatised or injured were not locked in cabins. They was taken to one of the restaurants what had been converted to medical stations. The medics tended to the wounds whilst us catering staff helped out with feeding them, changing the beds, things like that. Making sure they was comfortable. And it meant we got to talk to some of them. Those that could speak a little English.

'I don't want fighting,' one of them said, 'I am DJ, not soldier.'

WENDY

But, worrit was, we couldn't believe it when we saw the Argy officers strolling around ship like they owned the place.

Jeanie goes, ''Ere, he's gorra gun!'

And I told her, 'He's allowed, intee, being an officer and that.'

'Give over,' she goes, 'and worr if he decides to take revenge on us what have taken him prisoner?'

Well, I didn't have an answer for that, did I?

But some of those officers was educated at bloody Oxford and Cambridge and I couldn't believe the posh accent that came out of 'em. I mean, they'd got English what's better than mine.

KEITH

One of the POWs wouldn't let go of his backpack when he was ordered to. It had blood dripping out of it or summat, which made the marines open it up to check inside. Well, this Argentine lad tried to stop them, he was clearly hiding something, but they could never've guessed what. The lad had his brother in there. Or what was left of his brother after he'd been ripped apart by a shell or summat. It was just a head and shoulders basically, nowt else. But the lad wouldn't leave him behind. He was trying to bring the remains home to his family in Argentina for a proper burial, poor bastard.

MALLY

A couple of the prisoners kept on asking to go to the toilet all the time. And the state they came on board in we weren't surprised. The ship began to stink from the moment they came on. They had trench foot and all sorts of bugs, so we assumed these ones asking to go to the toilet had diarrhoea or summat. Turns out they were stuffing toilet paper into the vents in there to try and cause a fire so they could attempt to escape.

KEITH

For the first couple of days none of the prisoners would eat owt we served. We'd set up trestle tables for them on the car deck, unlocked their cabins, but none of them came out.

JOHN

They had all been told by their superiors, you see, that if they ever got caught then us Brits would either gas 'em or eat 'em! I s'pose it was their way of motivating them not to get caught, wunt it. So when they came on board via the car decks and saw all the shipping containers lined up there what held all our supplies, they was convinced these was gas chambers. And when we called them all onto the car deck for their tea they thought we was calling them down to put them in the chambers.

So, in the end, the marines went down and dragged a couple of 'em up to the deck and made them eat what we was serving. It was a bit rough, burr it was the only way to show them we wasn't trying to kill them.

WENDY

Quite the opposite, poor loves, we was trying to look after 'em, like you do, you know't I mean?

KEITH

So after that, they all came out and had a good feed, which was good to see.

Above left: Mally, more used to handling a ladle and chef's knife, tries his hand at shooting practice with members of 2 Para, May '82. The weapon is an L1A1 7.62mm self-loading rifle, known as the SLR, then the standard-issue assault rifle of the British Army.

Above right: Members of 2 Para during a physical-training session on *Norland*'s aft flight deck, May '82.

Below: Norland officers at firing practice: Back row, left to right: Frank Waller (Third Engineer), Allan Woof (Second Mate), Dave Risby (Second Mate), Chris Cammish (Second Mate), Bob Lough (Chief Officer). Front row: John Dent (Third Engineer), Lloyd Newell (Chief Engineer), John Crowther (Purser). Note the absence of their steward, Frankie 'Do I look like Annie Oakley?' Green.

Right: King Neptune and Queen Amphitrite (here played by Mimi) preside over the Crossing the Line ceremony, May '82.

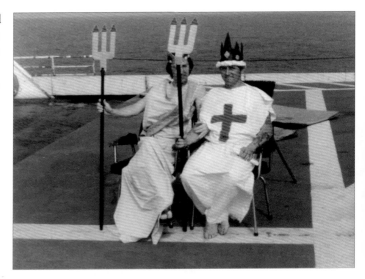

Left: Wendy with some of the lads from 2 Para in the Continental Bar.

Right: Mally in the ship's galley about to prepare barracuda for dinner, courtesy of the tropical waters off the West African coast, May '82.

Above: The Task Force heads for the Falklands, aiming to arrive in San Carlos Water by midnight on 20 May 1982.

Left: Wendy making sure the soldiers have 'something hot inside them' before they disembark on D-Day in the early hours of 21 May.

Right: The *Norland* in the midst of an Argentine air attack in San Carlos Water on the morning of 21 May 1982, just a few hours after she had put 2 Para ashore in landing craft.

Above: HMS *Antelope* passing close by *Norland* seconds after being bombed. The hole made by the bomb as it entered is clearly visible in the ship's side.

Below: *Antelope* is sunk in San Carlos Water, 23 May 1982. The *Norland* (in the foreground) is close by and receives survivors from the stricken frigate.

Above left: A young Brian in the radio room on board the *Norland*.

Above right: Wendy in uniform on the deck of the *Norland*, Port Stanley, June 1982.

Below: Frankie overwhelmed and underdressed ('always a scruffy cow') for the huge welcome awaiting the crew on their homecoming at Humberside Airport, 11 August 1982.

Top left: Don Ellerby, ship's Captain.   *(Photo courtesy and © Hull Daily Mail)*

Top right: Bob Lough, Chief Officer.

Below: Frankie Green and Jeanie Woodcock, photographed before the latter's death in 2008.

Above: Engineers working around the clock to fit one of two helicopter decks to the *Norland* in the dock at Portsmouth, April 1982.   (*Photo courtesy and © Hull Daily Mail*)

Below: The *Norland*, anchored in Port Stanley and looking a bit worse for wear after the Argentine surrender, June 1982. She is still in her original colours except for the funnel, which had been painted black with the insignia of 2 Para on it at the insistence of Colonel H. Jones. The two temporary helicopter decks fitted in Portsmouth are both clearly visible.

Right: 2 Para and *Norland* officers getting along famously, unlike their Navy counterparts at this point just south of Ascension, 9 May 1982. Left to right: Don Ellerby (Captain), John Crowther (Chief Purser), Tom Godwin (Captain Quartermaster, 2 Para), John Graham (Assistant Purser), Keith Thompson (Assistant Purser), Mal Simpson (Regimental Sergeant-Major, 2 Para). Foreground: Pengi, *Norland*'s mascot.

Left, left to right: Lloyd Newell, Bob Lough and Jim Draper at Government House, Port Stanley, with the Governor, Rex Hunt and his wife Mavis. Jim was the well-prepared chap with the NATO helmet, webbing and Mars Bars who hid under the sink in the pantry during air raids.

Right: left to right: Shep, Pete Samson, Reg Kemp, Mally and John with the *Norland* Bell and battle honours at the handover ceremony on MS *Pride of Hull* in June 2014.

JOHN

As they all lined up, I'd be putting a helping onto some plates and the kids would look at me all forlorn and hungry, like, and I felt sorry for them, so I'd sneak another helping on there.

WENDY

Oo, I did too. Especially to the few that was built like brick shit houses. You see I'm a twin. And my brother is a rugby player, believe it or not! And I know how much he eats. So when this bloke came up looking as big as my brother I put two helpings on his plate and that's when I heard:

'Oi, you!' It was one of the marines, having a go at me, 'Oi, you're giving them too much food. Stop giving them too much food. They're prisoners not bloody tourists.'

Well, I had a ladle in me hand at the time, dint I, and I was that close to whacking this marine over the head wirrit. Having a go at me in front of all the prisoners! Well, who the bleeding hell did he think he was, you know't I mean?

KEITH

I have to say, not all of them prisoners was happy with us though. As I was ladling soup into this one POWs bowl he sneered at me, 'If I escape I'm going to find you and hang you.'

Though it's no wonder some of them was aggressive. I mean, sometimes we'd see them getting dragged off down the alleyway, off somewhere to be interrogated. And I thought, there but by the grace of God go I, as I felt that ID card in my pocket, the one that we was supposed to give the Argies if we was ever captured. The one that said in big capital letters GIVE NO OTHER INFORMATION except your name and rank.

JOHN

That was the SAS that did the interrogating. They came back to the ship occasionally throughout the war, as quiet and closed off as ever. The only difference when they returned was how much they stank. My God, did they. Just like the POWs. Not surprising I s'pose when they'd been out in the field for days and weeks without so much as a wet wipe. If they wasn't interrogating prisoners they was sitting in the bar poring over documents, top secret information and plans. Then they'd disappear for another week as mysteriously as they came.

BOB

San Carlos Water – 7 June 1982

About five days after the first load of POWs came on board we were ordered to pick up another five hundred in San Carlos Water, then wait for cover of darkness to replenish with fuel and water from one of the tankers offshore before heading for Montevideo, the capital of Uruguay, to repatriate all the prisoners. As the war was still raging at the time there was no way we could go safely into Argentina itself so that's why we came to an arrangement with Uruguay. It was all arranged by the Red Cross and a condition of the voyage was that we removed all blackouts, put all the lights on and went unescorted.

WENDY

There was one prisoner we used to call Charlie. I have no idea why we called him that but, worrit was, he was easy to recognise because the poor boy had so many burns to his face that it looked like liver, raw liver, God love him, where a mortar bomb had gorrim. He used to sit in the corner like a rag doll, shell-shocked. But by the time we got him to Montevideo he perked up beautiful. His skin had started to grow back from all the nutrients he was gerrin from our food. We gave 'em these biscuits with loads of added vitamins, you see, and a nice bowl of stew and a cigarette. Oh, they ate as well as us, if not better, the prisoners.

KEITH

George, Mally and the rest of the cooks did an amazing job with what few stores we had left by then. We all agreed that George shurrav been given a medal as big as a dustbin lid for the dedication he showed what with making sure not just the prisoners, but the crew and the paras was well fed and well looked after throughout the war.

MALLY

Lieutenant Commander Coombs always came to the galley to inspect the food we was preparing for the prisoners. Inspect it to make sure it was of a high enough standard for 'em. And one day he saw the eggs we was using. Some of them had some black stuff on the shells, I don't know, from where they had been in the containers for so long, I s'pose, and he says, 'You can't use those. Use these ones only,' he goes, pointing to the ones that looked OK on the outside, 'Chuck those other ones out.'

'OK,' I says.

As if! I thought.

You see I knew all the eggs was the same. It was just a bit of shite on the outside that could easily be washed off. All the eggs, clean or dirty, was well over their use by date by now, technically, like, but I knew they'd be all right if we cooked them up well enough. Otherwise nobody would have had owt to eat. We was running so low on supplies it was getting pretty bad.

Commander Hughes came into the galley one day and asked me why they wasn't getting chips no more. Well, apart from the fact that when you're under attack the last thing you want to be doing is having the chip fryers on, full of hot oil, I says to him:

'I'd like to do chips for you, I really would, but the potatoes are no good.'

'Well, what about all of them there,' he goes pointing to a great big pile of 'em in the corner.

'They are only good for mash. I can do mash wirrem, but they're no good for owt else.'

'But I want chips!' he says.

So I says, 'You can't,' and I picked up one of the potatoes and squashed it with one hand, 'That's why,' I goes.

And Hughes goes, 'So when will I be getting my chips?'

Bloody hell! You'd think a commander might have more important things to worry about than whether he was gerrin chips or mash!

But things was getting so bad with the provisions that the ship's doctor had even come on the tannoy at one point and said:

'We need to conserve water badly so will all crew start drinking the booze instead.'

FRANKIE

Funnily enough I had gone right off booze since we'd first arrived in the Falklands. And off sex. I was too frightened. Remember, we all had our own cabins on *Norland*, but when there was an air raid threat we all had to go down to G deck, right at the bottom of the ship, and double up in cabins. And if there was a submarine threat then we all had to rush up to the top decks and double up there instead. On one of those submarine warnings one of the deck crew, who shall remain nameless, said to me, ''Ere, Francis, double up with me if you want to.' So I said thanks and I did. He was on his own bunk and I jumped onto his day bed. And that bloody klaxon is going off and I'm thinking, 'Fooking hell here we go again,' and he goes, 'Yer don't have to stay there, gerrin 'ere wimme.' Now he was supposed to be straight this one, but, as you know, there was a lot of half-poofs in the Merchant Navy, who, when they was away from the wives and kids, with no women around, didn't mind a bit of the other. So I look over at his bunk as he says this to me and I can see by the lump in his trousers that he's raring to go, and all I'm thinking is, 'How you can you think of that at a time like this!' Any other time, fine, you know, but not now.

In the days before the *Norland* I was on ships where you always had to share cabins. There just wasn't enough room, you see. I used to share with this girl called Judy and one night she had a gentleman visitor. I was on the bottom bunk and she was on the top bunk. If either of us met somebody that we fancied and brought them back to the cabin you'd put the curtain across your bunk, but you still had to listen to everything they was up to all night, you know. It was very rough that night she brought this chap back and the ship lurched to port and they both fell out of the top bunk onto the floor. They started laffing, but they could have killed themselves. And strangely his cock was still in her. At which point I opened my bunk curtains and said: 'Well, I've heard of giving a flying fook in my time, but this is ridiculous.'

BOB

With an enormous PW freshly painted on the funnel to indicate our new status as a prisoner-of-war ship, it took us four or five days to get to Montevideo.

Halfway up, in the middle of the night I got called out of bed by the second mate saying there was a man overboard. It turned out some marines and navy crew had been drinking in the crew bar and an argument had broken out between one of the navy boys and one of the marines, which wasn't unusual. All the different branches of the armed forces are notorious for rubbing each other up the wrong way. Anyway, on this occasion the navy guy had insulted the marine and the marine had chased the navy lad out onto the deck at the stern of the ship. To protect himself the navy guy had climbed outside the rails and shouted to his aggressor, 'Take one step closer and I'll jump overboard.'

Well, of course, this was just too irresistible to the marine who happily took one step closer and the other guy jumped.

We had a look out aft, keeping an eye on the stern, so it was immediately reported to the bridge and the ship was turned around. That's when I was alerted and went out in the rescue boat to pick up the casualty, who was lucky to be alive to be honest after some time in the choppy freezing waters of the South Atlantic.

Two years later I was at a Royal Marines dinner in Plymouth for the San Carlos Association. I was sat next to a navy officer and he asked me, 'What do you do?'

'I was first officer on board the *Norland*,' I replied, 'You?'

'Oh, I was commander on one of the nuclear submarines down there. I'm glad we've met actually as I always wanted to ask what on earth happened on your journey from San Carlos to Montevideo. We were your escort, you see.'

'We didn't have an escort,' I said a little mystified.

'Yes you did, we were underneath you all the way, but we couldn't communicate with any ships on the surface, of course, we had to remain invisible. You were heading north at around sixteen knots when suddenly you stopped, turned around and started zig-zagging all over the ocean causing havoc for us underneath, wondering why you were doing this crazy dance all over the surface.'

That's when I explained to him that we were trying to pick up this navy bloke who'd thrown himself overboard.

WENDY

Oo, he was a mad bastard, wuntee? A Taffy. A chubby Welsh bloke trying to throw kung-fu moves at this marine as he was chased down the corridor out onto the deck. It weren't easy to pick him up in those waters.

BOB

En route to Montevideo Jim Draper, second engineer (who you'd find under the sink full of water in the pantry, tin helmet on, beer barrels stacked all around him, during air raids) had the 4–8pm watch in the engine room. There was a toilet outside the control room there which is below the waterline and every time Jim used it he'd come back reporting this strange pinging sound.

'What's that pinging sound, Bob? Should we not be worried, Bob? Perhaps we need to evacuate, Bob?'

I, of course, pooh-poohed it as another of his conspiracy theories, another example of him being over dramatic. We'd all laughed at him, but that same navy submarine commander confirmed to me at the dinner in Plymouth that Jim was absolutely right. There would have been a pinging sound as the sub sent sonar up to the surface every so often to check on our position. Perhaps we shouldn't have mocked Jim so much.

COMMANDER TASK FORCE 317
COMMENDATION
Chief Officer R B LOUGH
MV *NORLAND*

Mr Lough is the Chief Officer of MV *Norland*, a North Sea ferry taken up from trade for the Falklands Operation. Throughout the deployment of the ship with the Task Force he gave tireless active support and thoughtful cooperation to the Military embarked personnel. He was instrumental in devising the method finally used for troop disembarkation during the initial landing phase. When the ship came under attack his courage and resolve were everywhere evident as he moved between decks – an example to the ship's officers and men.

Norland's only boats are GRP lifeboats designed to be launched from davits but requiring considerable skill for recovery. During the night of 10 Jun 82 on passage he lowered and took away a lifeboat to effect the successful rescue of a man overboard.

I commend him for his willingness, initiative and fortitude in ensuring the successful achievement of MV *Norland*'s task.

J Fieldhouse
ADMIRAL

BOB

The actual handover of POWs in Montevideo was organised with as much military precision as the landing of troops in San Carlos at the beginning of the war. And all under the auspices of international Red Cross representatives, one of which arrived on board in the early hours of 12 June.

KEITH

We made sure the prisoners had a good breakfast at nine o'clock that morning and each cabin was issued with one razor so they could shave, boot laces for each of them and access to the showers. Then they was ushered into the big Continental Bar where we kept the tea and coffee coming for 'em until it was time for 'em to disembark. It was there that this prisoner stopped me as I went past and I thought: 'Ere we go, he's going to lay into me now he's close to freedom, like that one what said he'd hang me if he ever got free.

But he didn't. He very simply, very warmly looked at me and said, 'Thank you. For everything.'

MALLY

It was at Montevideo that we was allowed under the Geneva Convention to take on supplies to make up for the provisions we'd used up on the prisoners, which was a godsend as we was really down to our final rations by then.

BOB

The Uruguayan agent who supplied the provisions was called Winston and when I went ashore to check these stores, which were in a lorry on the dock, he lifted a tarpaulin and there were a few cases of red and sparkling wine.

Winston smiled, 'A gift from Uruguay.'

It seems he did not agree with the Argentine claim on the Falklands.

9

TRENCH FOOT AND TENDERNESS

FRANKIE

14 June 1982

It was only a day or so after leaving Montevideo to head back to the Falklands when we heard the news.

I was having my afternoon sleep at the time. (In fact you're lucky to have me here this afternoon talking to you, as I should be having my granny nap right now!). Most of us was turned in, as we usually worked split shifts, early morning and evenings, unless the air raids was going. And suddenly *Land of Hope and Glory* comes blasting through the tannoy, really loud. Well, my nerves was shattered by now, frazzled, as you know, and I thought 'Oo, what's all this about now?'

Commander Hughes, one of the navy officers, you know the one what looked liked Christopher Biggins, came on and I thought, 'Oo, here we go again.'

But he says, 'A white flag has been raised over Stanley House, the Argentinians have surrendered. The war is over.'

JOHN

It was a frigging BBC journalist what reported the white flag being raised, so you didn't know whether to believe it at first. Those bloody journalists was always reporting things what they shouldn't have been. Lerrin cat out bag too soon, you know. Endangering troops like they had done when they reported that our paratroopers had broken through the beachhead and was heading for Goose Green, the silly bastards.

But this time it was right.

FRANKIE

So! Back on the piss, dear! We was all in the alleyways, me and Wendy and Mimi, all of us, crying, laughing, screaming, manic, cracking open the cans of Tennents. The cheer that went up from the ship that day must have been heard in Australia.

KEITH

It was more than a cheer. It was a roar. I was in my office at the time typing up the orders of the day or some other kind of administrative stuff. I heard the news on the tannoy and I dropped everything to run out on deck with the rest of the lads.

And when we sailed into San Carlos everything had changed. No more bombs, no more fear. The Harrier jets was doing a fly-by right over our heads. *Land of Hope and Glory* was blasting out the tannoy and it wasn't just 'the girls' getting emotional this time. All of us was in tears. There wasn't a dry eye on the ship as we all stood on deck in a way we hadn't dared to a week ago.

JOHN

All of us was hugging each other and saying, 'We're going home! We're going home!'

WENDY

Me and Jeanie had an extra shot of Bacardi each that day I can tell you.

FRANKIE

Me and Mimi went on a blow-job-athon to celebrate, dint we!

Margaret Thatcher (Prime Minister)

House of Commons – 15 June 1982

We do not need to negotiate in any way with the United Nations or anyone else about the British sovereignty of these islands. Our forces did not risk their lives for UN trusteeship. They risked their lives to defend British territory, the British way of life and the right of British people to determine their own future. I hope we have restored once again the dominance of Britain and let every nation know that where there is British sovereign territory it will be well and truly defended and will never again be the victim of aggression.

KEITH

The next day amid all the celebrations we made sure to think about those worrad lost their lives so we had a remembrance service led by the padre in the Continental Bar, the bar what was once bursting with Toms drinking and singing along to Wendy's piano. This time it was just the Royal Navy lads and *Norland* crew, all in our best bib and tucker, all paying our respects.

And then it all went a bit flat. The relief and the elation at thinking we was all going home turned into disappointment when we was told we would have to ferry more prisoners back to Argentina and not only that, but after we would be a garrison ship helping to ferry supplies and garrison troops back and forth from Ascension to the Falklands.

BOB

Norland proved to be just too useful, you see. And I'm quite sure that our War Orders, that agreement we made the navy commanders sign with us to keep everyone working so well together as we were heading south for the first time, I'm sure that was one of the reasons *Norland* was seen as such a useful asset and kept on.

KEITH

But I s'pose my feeling a little down wasn't just the fact that we wasn't going home soon. It was also the fact that I was feeling a bit queasy, which was unlike me. In fact, very quickly, feeling queasy turned to feeling bloody terrible and before I knew it I had stomach cramps and was vomiting all over the place. Before long it was coming out of both ends, I collapsed with a fever and the next thing I knew I opened my eyes to see fields and mountains rushing by below. The ship's medic had had me whisked off in a helicopter over to Stanley hospital on the Falklands. I was delirious by this point but I do remember waking up again in a nice warm bed in the little cottage with a handful of beds that passed for a hospital in Stanley. The army medics was there though setting everything back up since the Argentinians had left it in such a state. They hooked me up to a drip straight away and I stayed like that for a couple of days.

They was all calling it the Argentinian Bug. It was dysentery basically and I'd picked it up from the POWs because I was always in such close contact with them, making sure they was looked after and that. Unfortunately they had got all sorts of illnesses, being in the trenches like they had been, and they had passed it on to me. What with so many prisoners that loads of them had to be housed on the car deck, the toilet facilities there for 'em just had to be a very large oil drum, which soon stunk to high heaven. When it was full, just like them rubbish bags what we did target practice on on the way down, the contents would be tossed overboard, out the back of the open shell doors.

Anyway, three days after arriving at Stanley hospital, I was feeling much better so I told the doctors.

'Are you sure?' they goes.

And I said, 'Absolutely,' but I just wanted to get back to the ship so much that I might have said it even if I weren't. I was frightened she was going to set sail again without me, you see, and I couldn't bear that. Luckily I got there just in time before she was due to sail to Argentina.

WENDY

So after all the celebrations after the surrender, it was straight back to work coz, worrit was, HMS *Intrepid* brought us a thousand new POWs that needed shipping back to Argentina. And we had to go round to Port Stanley and get a thousand more un'all. Two thousand Argies crammed on a ship that was licensed to take a maximum of twelve hundred passengers. And some of them was in a right state, worse than the first lot. Trench foot, horrible wounds, emotional wrecks.

FRANKIE

Are you talking about them or us, love?!

SHEP

Now the war was over I thought it would be OK to take a few souvenirs home. Like one of them SLRs what we'd been firing off the arse end of the ship on the way down. Perhaps that's why this message went out to everyone.

TO: ALL CREW MEMBERS – MV *NORLAND*

YOU ARE REMINDED THAT IT IS AN OFFENCE UNDER CIVIL LAW AND THE NAVY DISCIPLINE ACT TO BE IN POSSESSION OF A FIREARM. ANY CREW MEMBER FOUND WITH A FIREARM IN HIS POSSESSION WILL BE DISMISSED ON THE VESSEL'S RETURN TO THE UK AND MAY BE SUBJECT TO CIVIL PROCEEDINGS.

   ANY PERSON WHO HAS A FIREARM IN HIS POSSES-SION SHOULD RETURN IT TO THE NAVAL OPS ROOM BEFORE 1600 THIS EVENING WHEN NO FURTHER ACTION WILL BE TAKEN.

18 JUNE 1982   D. A. ELLERBY
                 MASTER

SHEP

So did I go to the naval ops room at 1600 with that SLR in hand? Did I fook!

BOB

The reason the *Norland* was assigned to ferry all these prisoners back to Argentina was because we were a passenger ship and we had to enter Argentinian waters as such. As at Montevideo, no blackouts, all the lights on, sailing as a civilian ship under the watchful eye of the Red Cross.

JOHN

Two women it was from Red Cross. Both there to make sure we was complying by the Geneva Convention and that. And they said they had never seen POWs treated with such dignity and respect before.

Shame the same can't be said for the way they was treated back in Argentina. You see, when we arrived in Puerto Madryn there was lorries lined up on one side of the port and a marquee set up on the other. And the conscripts, the kids, as they filed off our ship was literally flinching and cowering as they passed by the Argy officials waiting on shore. As if they was expecting a kicking straight away for getting caught by the Brits. They was shoved into these lorries as if they was still prisoners in a way we wouldn't ever dream of doing and off they went to God knows where. Meanwhile the Argy officers we'd captured was saluted and ushered politely into the marquee for frigging tea and scones as far as I could see. It was bloody horrible for those kids, poor bastards.

KEITH

I had barely been allowed to go near the prisoners on the way to Argentina, let alone look after 'em, in case I caught something again, which was bad enough, burr it was very strict for all of us when we came into Puerto Madryn. None of us crew were allowed on deck, which was annoying coz we really wanted to say a proper goodbye to the prisoners.

WENDY

I was frightened going into Argentina like that. Well, worrit was, I mean, there was so many prisoners on board they could have easily taken over the ship if they'd wanted to, to be honest with you. Or, when the prisoners was all off, the Argies could've done something to us right there, with us all alone, away from the rest of the Task Force, you know't I mean? So when I went to bed in my cabin that night in the dock I said to Jeanie again, 'If I don't wake up then so be it. If they turn on us tonight, then I'll see you in heaven, love.'

JOHN

We wasn't the only ship taking POWs back to Argentina. The *Canberra* had to do it too. The difference was after she dropped off her prisoners she got to sail back to England and was given a hero's welcome. All that crew got to see their families and bask in all the glory while we was still ferrying supplies and troops up and down the frigging Atlantic.

BOB
Port Stanley – 24 June 1982
Around ten days after the surrender, we were anchored again in Port Stanley, the capital of the Falklands, and it was time for 2 Para, who we'd last seen when we landed them in San Carlos over a month ago, to embark so we could take them back to Ascension Island from where they would be flown home. But,

as you can imagine perhaps, they were in a lot worse shape than they had been when they left us.

KEITH

That was an emotional time for us all. It was great to see them all again and the funny thing was, whereas on the way down there had been some tension at first, even that soldier asking me why I let Wendy 'touch me up like that' when he saw her give me a hug, now it was the soldiers what was giving out the hugs.

JOHN

They was all running up to us and hugging us, cracking jokes with us and telling us how much they missed the *Norland*. Turns out they had been offered a ride home on the *Canberra*, but they had refused. Said they'd rather wait till *Norland* got back from dropping off the POWs in Argentina, just so they could go back with us, wunt it?

BOB

The *Canberra* is a beautiful luxury cruise liner. Two hundred and fifty metres in length, forty five thousand tonnes gross, its crew was nearly a thousand strong, whereas our crew was just a hundred. It could carry about two thousand passengers comfortably whereas we could only manage half that. She was cruising around the Mediterranean in April 1982 when she was requisitioned by the MOD and then was in and out of San Carlos Water, like us, landing marines and the third battalion parachute regiment (3 Para) as well as taking prisoners of war back to their homeland. The *Canberra* is nicknamed the Great White Whale, due to its sheer size and colour. It was an unmissable target for the Argentinians during air raids, but they tended to leave it alone as they did *Norland*, assuming we were just carrying supplies. Argentinian pilots have since claimed they were ordered not to touch *Canberra* as they thought she was a hospital ship. But, just in case, she was often anchored out of range of the Argentine air force in the Transport and Logistics zone, so consequently she came out of the war relatively unscathed.

The *Norland* by comparison was a bit of a state. Especially after all she'd been through. She'd taken a battering from the weather, was streaked with rust, she was grimy and could never have matched the *Canberra* for comfort anyway.

KEITH

But the boys of 2 Para had actually delayed their return home just so they could travel with us on the *Norland*. It seems the bond that we had felt growing between us was felt by them just as strongly.

JOHN

Some of them told us how they had been dug into the mountain-side, on Sussex Mountain it was, overlooking the bay at San Carlos after we first landed them and, even though they was getting shot at by Argies, they was looking at the bombs pounding the water around us below, watching the warships getting sunk left right and centre and saying, 'Please don't let the *Norland* gerrit. Please don't lerrem get bombed.'

WENDY

That Dave Brown, the lad what was twenty-one the night we purrem in the landing craft, he came back, thank God and he told us later how, as they was all cold and wet through, digging at the hard ground on the hillside to make a trench, that they said to each other:

'Look at them lot down there!' nodding to the *Norland* and all the other ships in the bay, 'They've got a hot meal, television and beds and we're stuck here.'

But as soon as daylight broke next day and they saw the air raids begin on the ships they said they was actually happy to be in them trenches. They might have been cold and wet, Dave said, but they could literally hide in their holes. For us there was nowhere to run to, you know't I mean?

That Dave went, 'We watched the *Norland* and thought, poor lads.'

JOHN

If you've taken a position as a soldier, you see, you know where the enemy is and you can fire back, but with them bombs you didn't know if it was going to hit the water or you, or the stern or the frigging bow or summat else.

FRANKIE

Oo, I was so happy to see them all back on board. I was so happy for them. But I was even more happy for me fooking self. Although I have to say the moment they came on board the ship stunk. They all had that terrible smell about 'em like what the Argy prisoners had when they came on board, so I said to one of the officers, 'What's that awful smell?'

And he goes, 'It's something called trench foot.'

'Trench foot?' I goes. And then I says, 'Oo, thank God it's on their feet and not on their nobs!'

JOHN

Any of the soldiers what came back on board for supplies or worrever when the Argies was still there, they would be pinching the POW's boots if they was in better condition than what theirs was to try and stop the trench foot. When 2 Para came back for good we didn't really see severe injuries among the lads. It was mainly that trench foot.

KEITH

And of course the mental scars what we couldn't see at first.

JOHN

I think the really badly wounded ones was taken off to special hospital ships like SS *Uganda*. She was a passenger and cargo liner that was requisitioned by the MOD and fitted out with wards and operating theatres, all proper hospital gear and that. She was painted white and had red crosses painted all over her, so she wouldn't be hit. I suppose that's what helped *Canberra* stay safe too, being so white and that. Medics on *Uganda* treated British casualties and Argentinian ones. Her call sign, if I remember rightly, was Mother Hen.

FRANKIE

Oo, did somebody call my name?

MALLY

Her call sign might have been Mother Hen, but what was ours then? Sitting bloody Duck, I reckon!

BOB

There was much cause for celebration now with the return of the troops and so we knew we needed to top up on supplies to make those celebrations swing. We usually got our supplies from the RFA supply ships. RFA stands for Royal Fleet Auxiliary. Civilian manned ships that support the navy all round the world. They are Merchant Navy that think they're navy. More navy than the navy, some of them. Can be a very officious bunch. Anyway, there was an RFA tanker in Stanley harbour which was supplying various ships via helicopter, and we didn't have any beer. With all these troops on board and all the celebrations that were about to kick off we knew we needed to stock up on beer desperately. What's more, Airborne Forces Day was only a few days away, so the celebrations were going to be doubly raucous where the paratroopers were concerned.

At five o'clock on the evening we were due to sail for Ascension Island I radioed through to the RFA ship in question and asked for some supplies of booze and I got this signal back from them saying:

'Very sorry but we've stopped flying for today, so we're unable to supply you.'

Getting my priorities right, I replied, 'Well, that's OK, we'll postpone sailing for today and we'll take supplies at first light in the morning when you resume.'

A signal comes back, 'Very very sorry, but we have other resources to supply.' Full stop, no more explanation, nothing.

Bollocks to that, I thought! Can you imagine sailing for nearly two weeks with a ship full of paratroopers who have an awful lot to celebrate and no booze? So I left word on the bridge before I turned in for the night saying, 'As soon as that RFA ship starts to up anchor get the engine started and give me a shout.'

Well it was only at eleven o'clock that night that I got the call that the supply ship was on the move. So we let go from the buoy and we followed her out of the harbour. We followed her all around the north of the island. The supply ship went back to San Carlos Water and anchored there and we anchored right alongside her. Not a word from the ship, radio silent. It eventually gets light, the sun comes up and a signal comes across from the supply ship.

'What are you doing here?'

I replied curtly, 'Waiting for the beer.'

There was another long silence until we heard the blades of the RFA helicopter start up and the beer arrived on the ship. So much for the RFA bullshit! Now we could sail for Ascension properly.

WENDY

Well, worrit was, as soon as the boys from 2 Para was back on *Norland* and we was headed for Ascension the carnival atmosphere returned. The piano was back out in the Conti Bar where the Toms drank, I was dressed to the nines in drag and we celebrated their safe return all the way back. It was Airborne Forces Day on the first weekend in July during our return journey, so on that day we partied harder than ever. Airborne Forces Day is like Christmas to a paratrooper so the tinsel what we had decorated ourselves and the piano with on the way down, the only thing we could find to give the stage a bit of sparkle, was more appropriate now than ever.

FRANKIE

Pressies was given just like Christmas. Captain Ellerby was given the helmet he had had to wear on the bridge during the bother to keep. I'm not telling you what I was given!

KEITH

That night Wendy had to play all three bars again – the Toms', the Sergeants' and the Officers' – and the big finale in the Toms' bar was packed to the rafters with the crowd chanting 'Wendy! Wendy Wendy!' And when she finished Regimental Sergeant-Major Mal Simpson…

WENDY

…the one that I had always thought was a right hard bastard, a right head banger, you know, in the early days when I saw him giving those poor boys hell for falling asleep in the sun and getting sunburnt…

KEITH

…he presented Wendy with one of the paratroopers' red berets. He was made an honorary paratrooper.

WENDY

In fact all the crew was made honorary paratroopers. It was quite overwhelming, wunt it. Jeanie was a proud as anything. All that parading round the deck in her enormous helmet waving that little Union Jack and singing 'Land of Hope and Glory'. It had all paid off as far as she was concerned.

KEITH

Captain Tom Godwin, who I had worked closely with organising supplies and that because he was 2 Para's quartermaster, he had returned safely and enjoyed the partying that night so much that when he got to his cabin he was so pissed he forgot about the raised metal doorstep on the entrance to each cabin and tripped and fell like a tree, whacking his face into the wash basin. He had two black eyes the next morning so when he landed in England a week or so later he just let everyone think it was a result of the action he'd seen on the islands!

WENDY

It wasn't *all* partying and singing on those nights after they returned. The lads from 2 Para had been through hell. They had seen some terrible things, you know't I mean? They had a lot to gerroff their chests.

JOHN

They told us about when the *Galahad* and the *Tristram* gorrit. About how they raced down to the shore to help the men stumbling in from the lifeboats. About the horrific burns, blokes holding out their arms with frigging ribbons of skin trailing down from their bubbling flesh. About how they rushed them up to the aid post telling them everything was going to be all right even though they knew it probably wasn't, but reassuring words was all they had.

KEITH

How when they gorrup close to the Argentines in the trenches they would have to chuck grenades in to kill them and how after they would see these Argentine guns with pictures of the Virgin Mary pasted onto the rifle butts. They realised then they was Catholic, just like some of the paras was. Just like a lot of us. They was tempted to feel sorry for them, to connect with them, but they knew they couldn't afford to do that. They would be killed if they did. It was kill or be killed.

JOHN

They told stories of gruesome sights: heads blasted off and faces with gaping holes in 'em. One man was still alive apparently, but his arms lay yards away from him on either side of the trench. Awful stuff like that.

BOB

We heard from Steve Hughes about another medic who completed a traumatic amputation on a soldier's leg on the battlefield on a forward slope in full view of the enemy, and in order to save the guy, this medic chopped off the casualty's leg with his Swiss Army knife whilst in total fear of his own life. He was awarded a Military Medal, quite rightly.

KEITH

RSM Mal Simpson told me how terrible it was when they was so low on ammunition he had to order his men to 'fix bayonets'. They literally had to stab the Argentinians. And of course when you do that you are right up close, inches away, not a hundred metres away like you can be with a gun; when you can tell yourself it's not really a person way over there you're shooting at, not really a young lad with a mam and a dad and perhaps a wife at home worrying just like you have.

JOHN

They told us about how some soldiers on the Argies' side raised a white flag behind the school house in Goose Green, so naturally when you see a white flag it means they've surrendered, dunt it. So the platoon commander and two other paras goes forward to take the prisoners. And as these three approached, the Argy bastards sprayed them with bullets and shot the three paras dead. Three of our boys. Not surprising some of our paras went nuts and wiped most of them out right there and then.

There was a lot of talk in the press and that for years after about these Argy bastards actually being Yankee mercenaries, fighting on the side of the Argies against the Brits. Now, I'm not saying it was true, but the ones that was taken prisoner, the ones that wasn't killed, was brought on board *Norland*, and I heard one of 'em shouting at our lot what had hold of him, 'Get off me you fucking limey bastard,' in a frigging American accent.

KEITH

Some official reports say that they was just Argentinians educated in the USA, so they had picked up North American accents. Perhaps that's true. We can only say what we saw and heard.

JOHN

You might have heard stories about some of our soldiers cutting the ears off Argentinians for trophies. Coming back to the ship with a pocketful of lugs.

WENDY

Oo, that's terrible, int it. Is that true?

KEITH

I don't think we even need to go into that here.

BOB

As well as 2 Para, this time we also had the third battalion Parachute Regiment (or 3 Para) with us on board. They came down originally on the *Canberra* and could have gone back on it too, but the powers that be realised they would be going back with one of the Marine Commando battalions. And you know how these different sections of the armed forces are so territorial, how they don't get on at the best of times, exemplified by that little spat between the navy lad and the marine which ended up with us trying to fish one of them out of the Atlantic on the way to Montevideo. Anyway, after a war, the tension was going to be even greater, so it was thought it would be best for 3 Para to travel back with some of their own kind: 2 Para. Little did they know how that would work out!

2 and 3 Para did not have to stay and form part of the garrison as the Prime Minister wanted a victory parade and these two battalions were ordered to be the star attraction, which they were all very happy about. But it reminded us that while all the celebrations would be going on back in an England bathed in summer sun, we would be left behind with the *Norland* beavering away in the freezing South Atlantic.

So between celebrations it was down to the business of sorting kit and equipment, debriefing and preparing the troops for home while the medics were busy treating the wounded.

KEITH

3 Para, they wasn't so happy to be coming back on the *Norland* like 2 Para was. They was on *Norland* without the connections like what 2 Para had made with us, and they'd missed out on going back in the luxury of the *Canberra*. So they started criticising our

ship, the food, the crew, having a go at Frankie, Wendy and the rest of the 'girls'.

'Who's the dirty little queer?' one of them said about Wendy when they was playing cards with some of the 2 Para lads. Well, the whole table turned on him.

'Look, mate,' one of 2 Para goes, 'He might be a queer, but he's our fucking queer, so unless you want your teeth rammed down your throat I'd shut the fuck up, all right?'

WENDY

I was playing in the Conti bar one night and all the 2 Para lads was singing along as usual. But some of the 3 Para was trying to ruin it, having a go, tekkin the piss, you know't I mean? And then an argument breaks out and soon fists start flying and then furniture starts flying. Well, it was just like bleeding Hessle Road on a Saturday night back in Hull, so what do I do? I keep on playing. I felt like the bloke on the piano in the saloon bars when the cowboys are having a brawl in those old westerns, you know't I mean? It was just like that.

KEITH

RSM Simpson came down and I said to him, 'Should we do owt, Mal? It's gerrin way out of control.'

And he just said, 'Get all your crew out and close these doors,' he said, pulling the big double door entrance to the bar shut. 'They just need to work it all out between themselves. Leave them to it.'

So we did. We sat around in the shopping area just outside the bar listening to things crashing and banging, smashing and knocking about. But what Mal was gerrin at was, even though they had been split up from the marines on the *Canberra*, they had been at war for a good few weeks, they had seen some horrific things, and they still had a lot of pent-up anger and aggression that needed lerrin out. And this was one way in which they was going to do it.

JOHN

I don't know what all the fuss was about. A few punches was thrown, a few things broken, it was nowt. I just carried on pulling pints as Wendy carried on playing 'Pack up your troubles in your old kit bag and smile, smile, frigging smile!'

KEITH

A good while later, half hour or so, I can't really remember, it all went quiet. And we opened up the doors to see the place wrecked. Chairs broken, glasses smashed, soldiers with chunks bitten out their ears or their noses. Blood everywhere. It was like we was back in the battle zone all over again. But the funny thing was it had seemed to do the trick as some of 3 Para had their arms around some of the 2 Para boys saying:

'Sorry I did that to you, mate.'

'I didn't mean it.'

'I have a lot of respect for you really.'

Stuff like that.

SHEP

That kept us carpenters busy for a few days anyway mending all that shit.

BRIAN

In between beating the shite out of each other the two battalions found the time and the heart to send a sweet message of congratulations to the Prince and Princess of Wales on the birth of their first wee son, who arrived into the world on the 21 June. And a few days later I received this message back from Buckingham Palace. Note the last line added by one of the royal signallers who sent the happy couple's message on to me!

82-06-25   15:47 from buckingham palace
to 2 para 3 para
all three of us send warmest and appreciative thanks to all ranks of the gallant 2nd and 3rd battalions for their splendid message. we can assure you that our son will not be called stanley.
charles and diana

He's going to be popular being called goose green, ain't he?

BOB

Ten days after weighing anchor in Port Stanley we arrived back in Ascension Island and disembarked both the paratrooper regiments so they could fly back home to England.

KEITH

It was sad to part ways with our 2 Para lads after all we'd been through, but we was happy for 'em to be going home. There was emotional goodbyes and lots of Polaroids being taken on deck before each soldier in an orderly fashion took their suitcase from the store area on the car deck where they had left it the day they had first arrived on board, nearly two months ago. As well as their kit bags they had had to bring a suitcase just in case they ended up being the garrison troops after the war was won and had to stay on down in the Falklands. Many of the soldiers were sad to be saying goodbye to us but they couldn't hide their excitement at the fact that they were not having to stay behind and knowing they'd be back home with their families in a matter of hours now.

I only wished I could say the same for myself. Here we was halfway home and we was going to turn round in a couple of days and sail right back to that barren place that had held so much terror and destruction for us. And that destruction hit us full on in the face as the last soldiers hurried off down the gangway for home and us crew what had been waving them off turned to see in the middle of the car deck a small pile of suitcases, unclaimed. Just eighteen of them. And since there was a thousand or so of them a few minutes before, this little pile looked so lonely there in that enormous empty space. It was the suitcases what belonged to the 2 Para boys that never returned from the war:

Lieutenant-Colonel H. Jones
Captain C. Dent
Captain D. A. Wood
Lieutenant Jim A. Barry
Sergeant Gordon P. M. Findlay
Corporal David Hardman
Corporal Steve R. Prior
Corporal Paul S. Sullivan
Lance-Corporal Gary David Bingley
Lance-Corporal Tony Cork
Lance-Corporal Nigel Smith

Private Stephen Jeffrey J. Dixon
Private Mark W. Fletcher
Private Mark Holman-Smith
Private S. Illingsworth
Private Tommy Mechan
Private David A. Parr
Private F. Slough

We had seen some things in our time down in the Falklands but never had we seen a sight as sad as those few suitcases standing all alone.

Captain Tom Godwin, 2 Para's quartermaster, had the sad task of identifying these cases and sorting through the personal effects in a quiet corner of the ship before making arrangements for them to be returned to the grieving families in England.

BOB

At this point I found myself recalling the planning meetings I attended with H. Jones and David Wood, during which they discussed how to deal with soldiers who would be killed in action. The plan was that they were to be buried where they fell and the position noted so their bodies could be retrieved later. At the end of the conflict a farmer from the island would be asked to dig a mass grave with a JCB from where the bodies could be eventually recovered. This was exactly what happened, however, it was David and H. who were the first to be laid in it.

MALLY

I couldn't help thinking back to that night in the galley when some of the 2 Para lads had been crawling on the deck outside pretending to be looking for summat when they was actually trying to pinch some of the joints of meat I'd just cooked, and how I'd had a guard put on the door after that. Well, what if them lads was some of the lads that never came back? As silly as it may sound, I felt really guilty then that they may have been out there feeling hungry when they was killed. I hate to think of them that way.

JOHN

I remember having a laff with that corporal in the bar about our pay. How we was gerrin five hundred quid a week to be down here and they was gerrin just a pound a day to be in the trenches.

'Well, when I come back,' he'd said, 'I'm going to come looking for you, John. And you can give me a handout!'

He knew me by name. I can't say I remember his. Everyone was coming to me to serve them behind the bar, you see, so they all got to know my name. But there was hundreds of 'em. I couldn't remember all their names. But I remember his face, that corporal. And I never saw that face again among all the troops we picked up after the surrender. Who knows, maybe he was one of the eighteen that didn't make it back?

10

FROM SEA KINGS AT DAWN TO MOWING THE LAWN

KEITH

Back in Ascension and out of the communications blackout, finally we was allowed to make calls to our families back home again. We was allowed to use the satellite phone on board, which Brian and the other Royal Navy radio officers took care of.

BRIAN

Our tight-arsed RFA friends passed on this notice to all the crew before they were allowed to use the equipment, though:

SATELLITE TELEPHONE RADIO CALLS
WHEN: IT IS EXPECTED THAT TELEPHONE CALLS MAY BE MADE FROM THE SHIP FROM JULY 2nd ONWARDS UNTIL OUR NEXT JOURNEY SOUTH (EXACT DATE NOT KNOWN).

COST: THE COST IS £5.11p PER MINUTE OR PART THEREOF.

PAYMENT: NAVAL PARTY 1850 BY CASH

SHIP'S COMPANY THROUGH SHIP'S ACCOUNT.

SECURITY

SECURITY IS STILL VITAL AND MUST BE TAKEN SERIOUSLY. THERE ARE SOME THINGS WHICH YOU MUST NOT TALK ABOUT:

• THE NAME OF THE SHIP MUST NOT BE MENTIONED
• THE SHIP'S POSITION
• THE SHIP'S PROGRAMME PAST/PRESENT/FUTURE
• OTHER SHIPS WITH US
• UNITS AND TROOPS EMBARKED
• WHEN YOU THINK THAT YOU WILL BE HOME

If any of these points slip out you will be immediately CUT OFF. YOU WILL STILL HAVE TO PAY. NO MORE CALLS WILL BE PERMITTED.

| A RICHARDSON | G J P WINGATE |
| 1st RADIO OFFICER RFA | UNIT SECURITY OFFICER |

BOB

Five pounds was a lot of money in 1982 and given how many things we weren't allowed to mention it didn't leave very much to say, so most of us didn't bother calling home at all. I got a bollocking back home for not calling or writing, but there was so much we couldn't say in a letter either, it hardly seemed worth it.

<u>OFFICERS AND CREW</u> MV *NORLAND*
MAIL FOR THE SHIP WHILE SHE IS AWAY
SHOULD BE ADDRESSED BY THOSE WRITING
TO YOU AS FOLLOWS:-
  MR ——
  MV *NORLAND*
  C/O NAVAL PARTY 1850
  B.F.P.O. SHIPS
YOU SHOULD NOTE THAT NORMAL U.K.
POSTAL RATES APPLY, I.E:
  FIRST CLASS 15½P
  SECOND CLASS 12½P

BRIAN

Some did pay their £5.11 to make a call and it was my job to set the calls up and monitor it all. It wasn't an easy thing to do and sometimes we were able to do it duplex, which is like a regular telephone call, or sometimes we had to settle for simplex, which is more like a walkie talkie, where you can't both speak at the same time. Anyway, one AB came in to make a call and I eventually managed to get duplex going which made things easier, but as soon as he got through to his wife all he could hear was their dog barking in the room as they tried to talk. He tried to get on with his conversation, but I was watching as his face became redder and redder, as he got madder and madder till eventually he exploded:

'For Christ's sake,' he says, 'Gerrid of that dog! I dint pay five pound a minute to talk to that fooking animal.'

SHEP

We bunkered up at Ascension with water and oil and got more stores of food on board ready for the journey back down South. This was in our new role as South Sea Ferry. And our first passengers were the Queen's Own Highlanders, who were forming part of the garrison as well as a small bunch of Falkland Islanders what had fled as the troubles began and could now return home. Although why they would want to go back to such a pimple on the arse on the earth I have no idea.

BOB

We officers had been going ashore occasionally for all sorts of reasons, but the likes of Frankie Green and the rest of the stewards hadn't set foot on dry land for over two months and so not surprisingly they were desperate to get off for a spell now. I was determined to make it happen for them, to get everyone a lift ashore in one of the helicopters so they'd have a break from the ship, but the swell was so great at the time that the ship was rolling all over the place, so much so in fact that the helicopters couldn't land on or take off from the flight decks safely. Undeterred I found a solution, which was to up anchor and steam up and down in the lee of the island with the stabilizers out which kept the ship level and the helicopters could do their job of shuttling people back and forth to land.

BRIAN

Ascension Island – 7 July 1982

I went ashore in Ascension that day by Sea King helicopter and walked round the village of Two Boats. I met a BBC fella living there who asked me back to his place for a beer.

The next day saw Naval Party 1850 leaving the ship, so at last we were back to one captain, one crew, the way it should be, and the following day the ship sailed for Port Stanley again with the Queen's Own Highlanders, about thirteen Falkland Islanders returning home, and journalists from the BBC and ITV.

KEITH

It should have been more relaxed, more of a laff, perhaps, taking these troops down to a secure environment than it ever should have been ferrying frightened, angry, aggressive, battle-ready soldiers and prisoners around a war zone, but it was all a bit flat really. The relief we had felt after the surrender was now replaced with a low, probably coz we had been running on so much adrenaline for so long. And because we was ready to go home, but we was sailing in the opposite direction. Although Wendy still did her best to keep our spirits up as usual.

WENDY

I was glad some Falklanders was on board coz some of them was women and I was able to borrow a dress from one of them for my drag act. I was getting a bit tired of wearing the same old thing every time I played, you know't I mean?

KEITH

The Purser Department was a great team of shipmates. It consisted of John Crowther (Chief Purser), John Graham (Assistant Purser, like me) and Harold Sutherland (Shop Manager). The day we left Ascension we received this letter, which was so lovely, but made the journey back down south even more heartbreaking, if you see what I mean.

M.V. *Norland*
Tuesday 8 July 1982
Ascension Isles

Dear John, John and Keith,

My handshake was not enough to express the gratitude that I have for you all. You may not have realised it but only for your willingness and understanding efforts, our initial landing at Port San Carlos could have been different to what it was. The men disembarked leaving behind them a real sense of affection for the ship and its crew. This we all carried with us during battles and whilst on shore. It was this memory that we referred to when thinking of our return home and one which never left us. Please accept once again my thanks on behalf of so many of us for what you all did. We shall never forget. A safe journey home.

God Bless to you all,

Del Amos,

2nd BN, PARACHUTE REG

FRANKIE

Port Stanley – 19 July 1982

We offloaded the Queen's Own Highlanders and the locals, and when we had finished our work for the day we were allowed to go ashore again. And where was the place most of us headed to first? The pub, of course!

JOHN

The Globe was one of three pubs in Stanley. There was the Rose and the Victory too, but the Globe was closest to the jetty so it was a shorter distance to stagger for the last boat back at closing time. Coz of that, it had never seen so much business in its entire existence as it saw in them weeks after the war. The landlord was obviously happy with that but most of the locals was happy to have us there too.

SHEP

Some of us used to call the islanders Bennys. After Benny on *Crossroads*, what everyone watched on telly in them days. Because they all wore those tea-cosy hats like what Benny wore and they all seemed to be a bit daft like him too. Course, when MOD got wind of this, a message came down from on high warning us not to be tekkin the piss.

JOHN

I was having a drink in the Globe on that first day ashore and I looked out the window and saw out the back there was a frigging mountain of rifles out there. Argy rifles as it turns out, all chucked there after they'd been confiscated from the POWs. And a few days later all these rifles was loaded onto *Norland* and she sailed with them next time she went out to open water. When the water was deep enough the car doors was opened and this mountain of guns was pushed out and into the deep. Worra waste!

FRANKIE

Port Stanley was a Godforsaken place. I mean no offence to the islanders, but it was barren at the best of times, and after the bother it was even worse.

JOHN

There was a stench of burning and another smell what I couldn't put my finger on. I can only say it must have been the stink of death. There was big plastic sheets covering up things by the roadsides. I never found out what was under those sheets, but it might well have been bodies. There was a strong smell of shit un'all, which wasn't surprising when we heard the Argies had literally gone into the locals' homes when they had invaded and shat on their beds. The islanders was having to clean human shite off their stuff for weeks after. There was smashed windows everywhere and holes in the sides of some houses from mortar bombs so you could see right through to the living rooms. One of them bombs had killed three ladies. The locals what was killed during the bother.

Mrs Susan Whitley
Mrs Doreen Bonner
Mrs Mary Goodwin

They was killed by British shelling (frigging 'friendly fire') when they was sheltering in a house together as our navy bombed Stanley.

WENDY

The whole place looked like it had been trodden on, you know't I mean? They was proud people the islanders, but worrit was, the Argies had left a right mess behind and the islanders looked trodden on too.

From a distance you've got the rooftops of the town all different colours: red, brown, green, baby blue, all quite pretty sprinkled about the hillside, but as we got closer…Well, right in the harbour there was the *Sir Tristram*, nowt more than a hunk of twisted metal now, full of black gaping holes. And the *Yorkshireman* tugboat standing next to it seemed to be holding the wreck up, you know't I mean? It seemed to be the only thing stopping the warship from sinking.

BOB

I think that is just about right. The *Sir Tristram* was a landing ship and while we were transporting prisoners-of-war to Montevideo back in early June, she was transporting troops and supplies round to Fitzroy Cove on the other side of the East Island to San Carlos, just south of Stanley. It was 1400hrs on 8 June when she was attacked by Argentine Skyhawks. Her decks were strafed and two crew members killed. A five-hundred-pound bomb penetrated the deck but failed to explode straight away giving the rest of the crew time to evacuate. When the bomb did go off the ship was abandoned, but later used as an accommodation ship in Port Stanley right up until 1984 when she was put on a heavy-lift vessel, transported back to the UK and extensively rebuilt.

The Sir *Galahad* was with her that day in June, but unfortunately did not come off as well. Back on 24 May, when we were sitting among all the explosions in San Carlos Water and the *Antelope* was sinking, *Galahad* was strafed by Dagger fighter bombers and penetrated by a thousand-pound bomb, which, like the one that hit *Tristram*, did not detonate but was later safely removed. She then did supply runs until 8 June when she was landing the Welsh Guards near Fitzroy. As the Skyhawks attacked, *Galahad* was hit by two or three bombs and set alight. In the fierce fires and explosions that ravaged the ship forty-eight crewman and soldiers lost their lives. In order to survive the infernos and the thick black smoke, some men jumped overboard but met their fate in the freezing waters or the burning oil floating on the surface.

WENDY

Simon Weston was among the Welsh Guards injured in the fires that day. And most people know how badly he was burnt with his face hardly recognisable after, God love him.

JOHN

Well, the *Sir Galahad* was carrying thousands of gallons of fuel and ammunition, wunt it, just like we was on the arse end of *Norland*. Thank God we never gorrit otherwise we would have gone up just like she did.

BOB

When the Argentinians had been expelled from the islands they had left an awful lot of equipment behind, including some brand new Mercedes jeeps, the original G-Wagen, lying about everywhere. So everybody was commandeering them, the Scots Guards, the Paras, the military police, they were all driving around in these flashy jeeps.

RAF 18 Squadron had been living on *Norland* since the beginning but were now based in San Carlos settlement. They had lost all their original Chinooks when the *Atlantic Conveyor* went up in flames, taking all the aircraft on board with it. But they had been re-supplied with new helicopters to fly troops from us as we brought them back from Ascension to various locations around the islands.

I was on the bridge one day after we had sailed round to San Carlos Water when a message came through with an invitation to lunch with Wing Commander Staples, the boss of 18 Squadron.

'I would love to come to lunch,' I answered, 'But unfortunately I have no way of getting over at the moment.'

'Not a problem,' came the swift reply, 'We'll send a Chinook.'

'Wow, I'm honoured,' I thought. But then I also thought, 'You know the saying: there's no such thing as a free lunch. What's this all about then?'

Nevertheless when the Chinook landed on the aft of the ship I jumped in and went for this lunch in San Carlos settlement.

Lunch with the Wing Commander! Caviar, followed by duck à l'orange and a nice sorbet to finish? No, lunch consisted of John Smiths beer and tinned sausages with a slice of bread.

And the bottom line, when Wing Commander Staples finally came out with it, was that 18 Squadron had commandeered on of these G-Wagens, like everyone else. They had also just got instructions that they were about to be repatriated the following month, so they wanted me to take their Mercedes jeep on the *Norland* to Ascension Island for them on our next run north.

'Well, I would love to help you, of course,' I told the Wing Commander (especially after such a wonderful lunch!), 'But I can't really do that as we have had strict instructions from General Thorne,' who was Commander of the British Forces, the big boss on the ground in the Falklands, 'that no equipment is to be removed from the islands.'

'Ah,' said the Wing Commander knowingly, 'I understand, but my boss in London outranks General Thorne, so it won't be a problem. It is totally fine for you to transport this jeep for us.'

'OK. If you say so,' I said.

And soon enough the jeep was delivered to us by Chinook in the middle of a blizzard and we put it onto the car deck and began our next run north on July 31st, which was taking the Scots Guards home.

During the run up to Ascension some of the Scots Guards found this jeep. They had wanted to paint some of the car deck and turn it into a squash court and that's when they came across the Mercedes, at which point they stole the keys and reported back to General Thorne that we were removing equipment from the islands.

All hell broke loose. There was a big row between us and the officers of the Scots Guards which didn't make the twelve-day trip to Ascension too pleasant.

I demanded the key back for safety reasons.

'It's my ship,' I argued, 'And I'm responsible for the safety of everyone on board her. We cannot have a vehicle on the car deck without an accessible key.'

This worked, but the Scots Guards were going to keep a firm eye on that jeep. So once I had the key in my clutches I decided to have an abandon ship drill, which everyone on board has to attend. Everyone that is except the men I'd organised to take the jeep one deck below the car deck, park it up inside one of the many now empty shipping containers and lock the container. When the Scots Guards returned from the drill to watch the jeep it was gone. And they never did find it.

When we finally arrived at Ascension, RAF Ascension's Chinook flew over and removed the jeep. The last we saw and heard of it was when it was put on board the five-thousand-tonne merchant ferry *Tor Caledonia*, which was heading north, back to the UK.

At least, I thought that was the last I was going to hear of it.

KEITH

On our arrival in Ascension we was given the news that finally we was allowed to go home on leave.

JOHN

But not all at the same time, which upset a lot of people. We all wanted to arrive home together, just as we left but we was told we'd have to go in two groups.

KEITH

It was a hard decision to make for the heads of departments, but that was how it was done in the end. Captain Ellerby went back with the first lot, leaving Bob to step up as captain. Frankie, Mimi, Shep, Bill, Shirley and Jeanie all went back with the first lot too. Wendy, me and John stayed. It was another really emotional time seeing most of our crew, the team we had gone through so much with, leaving us behind, but we also knew that we would be going home soon enough, which was a wonderful thought.

When we dropped off the guys in Ascension a relief crew was ready to board. They brought letters with them from our families back home, which was lovely, but there wasn't too much time to get sentimental as it was straight back to work the next day, business as usual, training up the new crew and that. When this crew arrived on board they was totally unused to the situation of the ship. People like Bob, Dave and a couple of the engineers stayed with us on board to introduce the new lads to the way the ship was now operating.

WENDY

I was meant to go back on the first chalk with Frankie and Mimi and that, but, worrit was, there was a father and son in the crew and one of them was in the first group, but there wasn't enough room for them both to go back together unless someone else gave up their place on the first lot. So I did, you know't I mean?

BRIAN

We arrived at Ascension at 9.30pm on 8 August and disembarked the Scots Guards. The relief crew for the *Norland* flew into Ascension at 9pm the following day on a VC10 from the UK and they joined the ship at 11pm by helicopters. I spent the 10th going over gear and so forth with my relief and, as there were no spare cabins on board now, I slept on a mattress on the radio room deck.

The next morning I woke at four in the morning and was on a helicopter by five flying to Ascension airport, known as Wideawake Airfield because of a very noisy colony of sea birds that lives nearby. I took off in a VC10 at 7am with the rest of the crew that were leaving. It was a three-hour flight to Dakar, Senegal. We stopped over for an hour to refuel, then took off for the six-hour flight to RAF Brize Norton. We landed at 7pm and were met by North Sea Ferries management and a crowd of well-wishers. We had to go through customs and met press and TV. We left again at 8.15pm on a chartered Viscount to fly to Humberside airport. We landed at 9.30pm to a big welcome from radio and TV and hundreds of people. Liz and the children were there and we went straight home in a car with chief engineer Lloyd and his wife. That was a total of 113 days away. And that last one felt like one of the longest. It was so nice to be home.

At first it was hectic with civic receptions, special meals, get-togethers and so forth, but we soon settled down to normal life again. Paying the bills, cutting the grass, sorting out the kids. Having spent a lifetime at sea I really enjoyed home comforts when I was there.

Unlike the rest of the crew, radio officers were not employed by North Sea Ferries, but by Marconi. We tended to move around from ship to ship, while the crew tended to stick to one. We were also on a different leave system (two months on, one month off), so my relief in the South Atlantic knew he was there for two months when he embarked at Ascension.

I had a month at home, but then it was time to go back to work, so I joined the Norwave on the Hull–Zeebrugge run on 29 September 1982 and it was back to normal. The odd passenger spotted your Falklands ribbon on your uniform and would say well done and all that, but it soon faded.

FRANKIE

I flew with Brian and the rest from Ascension to RAF Brize Norton in Oxfordshire and from there we took another plane to Humberside airport. As we're coming in to land the hostess points out the window and says, 'Well, boys,' she says, 'Looks like you have a bit of a reception down there waiting for you.'

So we all peer out through the little windows and I can see 'em all by the runway, a big welcoming committee of families. Well, I didn't expect that and I wasn't ready. I mean, I was always a scruffy cow, you see, always in a vest. I leaned over to Mimi and said, 'Are you seeing this?'

'Oh my God,' Mimi goes, 'that's wonderful, int it?'

And there's me thinking we'll just go home and have a nice pot of tea, like Hinge and Bracket would or summat, you know, but this was wild. My mother was there and all my brothers and sisters, coz I have a huge family I do. *Huge!* It was crazy, but it was lovely.

And when all the celebrations and family dos were over, and me and Mimi was back in the little house we shared in Albert Avenue, it was so weird. I mean, I was made up to be home, to be away from all the bother, but I missed it somehow too. My crew mates and the boys from 2 Para, the bonds, you know, what can only form between people thrown together into such extreme conditions.

KEITH

Two weeks after Frankie, Brian and the others had gone it was the rest of us turn to go home. We flew, just like Frankie did, to Brize Norton and then onto Humberside. A coach then took us into Hull. That whole journey seemed to take forever, especially the last leg, the closer we got. It was midnight when I finally knocked on the door of my house, in a terrace in the west side of Hull, a million miles from the world I'd inhabited for the past few months. My two daughters, who'd been struggling to stay awake to see their dad, was suddenly full of beans and bowling down the stairs hysterical with happiness. Jayne, my wife, was teary to say the least. We was all hugging on the doorstep so much it took ages for me to actually get over the threshold, but once I did it was so good to be home. To be surrounded by my own things, to hear the sound of children and be with my wife, to be in the company of a *woman*, all rare commodities on a Merchant Navy ship!

WENDY

There was parties everywhere when I got home. A lot of the places I used to play put on a party for me. The Albion, the King

Billy, the café on the pier. And then I'd be playing the piano of a night to raise money for the South Atlantic Fund what helps veterans of the Falklands. It was non-stop!

But when it came time to go back down there again I wasn't bothered. I didn't dread it, you know't I mean? Well, I knew the war was over, it couldn't be any worse than it had been, now could it?

11

COLLAPSING UNDER THE STRAIN

DAVE

We kept shuttling troops and supplies back and forth to Ascension until October when the *Norland* finally needed some attention. The bearing ran hot. That is, the main bearing on the crankshaft, which drove the pistons, overheated and she needed some serious repairs, which meant we would have to be anchored in Port Stanley for nearly a month whilst we awaited the parts and whilst the work was done. Because of the very changeable weather conditions down there (one minute it would be bright blue sky and sunshine, the next it could be snowing with a hurricane) and the high superstructure of this relatively light ship of ours, she had a tendency to drift at anchor, as Bob mentioned before when that bomb would have hit us if we hadn't have drifted. So whilst the repairs were being done we decided the best thing to do would be to secure the ship to a buoy in the harbour. And guess whose job it was to do the tying? Muggins here!

We had seconded to us at this time an army major. Let's just call him Major M—. Major Disaster more like, who liked nothing more than buzzing around the harbour in an inflatable, his pride and joy. So he couldn't wait to take me out to the big mooring buoy poking out from the cold water, whilst one of the anchor chains was run out of the *Norland* without the anchor on. A strong rope was then passed through the end of the chain instead of the anchor itself and the rope would then be handed down to me so I could pass it through the eye of the buoy and back onto the ship. Then an enormous shackle and pin would be attached to the chain on the buoy and filled with lead shot to keep everything in place. We didn't have the necessary shackle until we went on board the wreck of the *Tristram* and 'borrowed' theirs.

So one of the ABs, myself and Major M– went out in his bloody dinghy to the buoy. The wind was quite strong that day, so the *Norland* was shifting about a lot as it got near to us, but Bob was doing his best to keep her steady. The AB got onto the buoy and I was hanging over the bow of the inflatable, fiddling with the shackle, lead shot and hammer in my pocket ready to bang it in securely, while Major M– pushed the dinghy up against the buoy to hold it there. Until that is he decided, for some reason I'll never understand, perhaps because he couldn't stay still in that bloody dinghy for too long, he backed away from the buoy. And of course, I fell straight through the gap, into the icy water.

BOB

In order to make best use of the ship while we were having the repairs done we became an accommodation ship for that month, with various small units of military personnel staying on board.

But we all knew by then how different branches of the forces rubbed each other up the wrong way; how they tended to fight and thieve each other's gear. This was going to need a bit of policing. So without the marines on board anymore now the war was over, we sent for our own ship's policeman, who usually did the security patrols on board, and invited the police force of the Falkland Islands over, which numbered one constable.

DAVE

Even so, there still wasn't a great deal for them to do, or for us to do for that matter. The ship was going nowhere so to be on watch from midnight to six in the morning it was a matter of put your feet up and close your eyes until you'd hear over the radio the ships starting to communicate with each other at five thirty in the morning, the highlight of which would be when the milkmaid came out to milk the cows on the hillside and various hairy-arsed sailors could be heard, eyes glued to binoculars, going:

''Ere she comes!'

'What's she wearing today?'

'That lovely mac again. I swear she wears that just for me.'

BOB

So we gave our policeman a quick briefing on how to run a bridge watch, how to use the communications equipment, sat him in the Captain's chair and he loved it. It was the making of the man. And it gave us all a bit of a breather too.

DAVE

When you sail into Port Stanley you have to pass between two headlands and the gap is quite narrow. A Danish ship came in early one of those mornings. Knowing the way our ship used to drag in the winds we didn't want the Danish one anchoring too close to us, so Bob suggested I go aboard her and show her the best place to anchor, since we had been here longer than just about any other ship and we knew the waters far too well by now. So I shoved a chart under my arm and buzzed across in the boat. I moved their ship two hundred yards for them and said:

'There you go, Captain!'

'Thank you very much,' he said, 'Schnapps?'

'Oh, don't mind if I do,' I said, even though it was five o'clock in the morning.

A few glasses and God knows how much time later I could hear Bob's voice coming out of the VHF radio, 'Dave? Dave? Are you all right? Are you on your way back?

'Dave?

'Dave…?'

WENDY

I had a lovely time going ashore while the ship was in Stanley. Worrit was, I had got chatting to some of the locals when we was bringing them back from Ascension, and, like I say, even borrowed a dress from one of 'em for my drag act. So when they was back on their feet on the islands they would invite us over for tea. There was this one girl called Claudette, who was one of the DJs on the radio station in Stanley, another called Rhonda, I think, whose mum worked in the general store, she was a singer and played guitar, so us three had a lot in common when it came to chatting about music and that. And the matron at the hospital. I forget her name, but I remember her face when I brought her a bag of fruit from the ship. Anyone'd think I had brought her a bag of gold, you know't I mean? Well, worrit was, you see, they couldn't pop over to Buenos Aires anymore like they used to and go on shopping trips over there where everything was cheaper. The Argies didn't welcome them anymore, of course, so a bag of fruit *was* gold dust, wunt it?

BOB

The original runway at Port Stanley had now been extended so that Phantom combat jets could take off from there. There were Vulcan Tankers flying around above to refuel them, which the Phantoms had to rendezvous with immediately after taking off so that they would have enough fuel to carry out their patrols. Bombers such as Phantoms and the Skyhawks the Argentinians were using consume fuel incredibly quickly. They can achieve a shorter take-off roll if they carry less fuel, i.e. less weight, on the runway, but that means they have to refuel once airborne. Also they can take off with a greater payload (the carrying capacity of an aircraft), which in this case would be bombs, personnel and so on, if they have less fuel on board to begin with, again refuelling once in the air. The only trouble with this was our position in Stanley harbour was directly underneath the point where, just after take-off, the Phantom pilots would pull their stick back and put their afterburners on to gain the altitude necessary to reach the Vulcan tankers. The resulting noise shook the ship. It was quite incredible. It felt like we were in an air raid all over again every time!

WENDY

Sometimes, while we was in Stanley, some of the big cheeses from the Falklands came over to the ship for dinner and drinks with the officers. And while Frankie was on leave they had the governor of the Falklands, Rex Hunt, and his wife Mavis over. And coz Frankie wasn't there they was one short so they asked me to come up and serve dinner for 'em in the saloon. Well, I can't be doing wirrit usually, all that posh stuff, but I did my job that night and got so into it I felt like I was back in the old days, you know't I mean, and I had all these images of HMS *Victory* and Nelson running around my head (from that night in Portsmouth when we got pissed up on the free bar), that I ended up calling Mavis, the governor's wife, Lady Hamilton. I just came out wirrit, couldn't help myself! But I think she saw the funny side.

FRANKIE

South Atlantic – 23 December 1982

Me, Jeanie, Mimi, and the rest had just had our two weeks of Christmas leave and got back on board *Norland* at Ascension, sailing for the Falklands once again. Keith, John and the others with kids and that then went off for their two weeks over Christmas itself, you know. Captain Ellerby hadn't come back since that first time we went on leave, though. I think his nerves was as frazzled as mine after all the bother and he needed a good rest, bless him.

Captain Derek Wharton was the relief captain who came down this time to give Bob a break, so he could go home. Derek Wharton was a Geordie, a lovely man. He used to call me his personal poof. I knew him of old. I had been his steward on many a trip when he was relieving Captain Ellerby in the past, long before the war, you know. I'd wind him up just like I used to the other officers and, although he'd tell me off for it, he secretly loved it. I knew it because I'd overhear him telling the other officers about how I'd tekk the piss out of him and that.

Anyway, as well as our crew we had some other merchant seamen what we was bringing back from leave and some soldiers what was coming down to the Falklands as part of the garrison, you know. So we was all having a drink in the Continental Lounge one night, all good fun as usual, getting in the Christmas spirit (or rather drinking all the Christmas spirits), as well as you can when you're back on the arse end of the earth again. But everyone was having a good laff, a good party and I goes for a wee, as you do. Now, I should say here, that one thing I am not, I am not a groper, drunk or sober, I do not go around grabbing men, straight or gay, and making a nuisance of myself. Not like my mate Terry. He was down as part of the relief crew and I'd already bought him a T-shirt from the shop on board with an octopus on it! Couldn't keep his hands to himself that one, God love him. He came running to me one day and said, 'Oo, Frankie, would you do me stint for me today serving breakfast behind hot plate?'

'I can't, love,' I goes, 'I've got my own work to be doing. Why, what's the matter, are you poorly?'

'No, it's not that,' he goes, 'I just went groping a squaddie last night when they was asleep and if he recognises me at breakfast this morning he might bray me 'ead in.'

'No! I am not doing that,' I says. 'I'm not gerrin involved.' Coz that just wasn't my style, you see.

Anyway, back to this night at the party in Conti Bar, as I come back from having a wee two squaddies jump out from behind a fire door and drag me down an alleyway, one of them saying, ''Ere's the fooking queer.'

'Are you the cunt that plays the fooking piano?' the other one goes.

Terry had seen this happen and he was there shouting, 'No, it isn't! He doesn't play the piano! Wendy's not even on the ship. She's gone on leave!'

But they wasn't listening by now and they kicked me to fook. Just for being a poof. Black and blue I was. *Black and blue.* Well, I've never been hit in my life, not even by my parents. I remember the first whack. But then I conked out. I don't remember anything after that until I woke up, pain all over my body, in this dark alleyway near deck aft. And I just ran. Down to the freight deck, along and down to my cabin on G deck where I locked myself in.

The next thing I know, the night steward, Reg Kemp, was banging on my cabin door, coz some of the other squaddies had said to him, 'One of your crew members has been filled in and we think they've thrown him over the side.' At which point Reg had gone spare, rang the bridge and told them to stop the ship.

'Well, what are you bothered about?' these squaddies were going, 'It's only a queer.'

Sounds like something from the 1940s, I know. After everything we'd been through in the early days when 2 Para was getting used to us, and us to them, and then surviving the war itself without so much as a fooking scratch, and when all the bother is over I get more hurt than I ever had in my life. And for what?

When Reg was sure I was in my cabin and not overboard I heard this message come over the tannoy from Captain Wharton for me to come to his cabin, which I wasn't happy about coz I was so embarrassed to be seen so bruised up, not to mention frightened still. But I guess Captain Wharton didn't know just how bad it was until I walked into his cabin and he goes:

'Good God!' he says, 'We're going to find out who did this, Francis,' he said.

'Captain,' I sighed, 'Even if you did, all they're going to say is I tried to touch them up or summat. Gay bashers have been saying it for thousands of years to justify what they do and gerrin away with it.'

'Well, they won't get away with it this time, Francis, because I know you. I know you very well.'

I went back to my cabin and I stayed there for ten days without coming out. I was too frightened to. And when I was in there Captain Wharton announced over the tannoy:

'Hear this! Hear this! If nobody comes forward and admits to what they have done to one of my stewards then *all* army personnel leave will be cancelled.'

And with that they came forward. Or rather they'd have been pushed forward by other squaddies what didn't want to lose their leave. I don't know exactly what happened to them, but I said to Captain, 'I bet they said I was trying to grope them, dint they?'

And Captain goes, 'Look, I just want to drop it now, Francis. I want you feeling better and I want you back to normal.'

'Well, Captain,' I says, 'I can't see that happening, can you? Me? Normal?' I couldn't resist a little joke, you see, even at a time like that.

'You know what I mean!' Captain says trying to hide a grin.

KEITH

It was so awful to hear about Frankie when I got back from leave. I was angry. I was disgusted. It was painful enough tearing myself away from my family after a couple of weeks at home at Christmas, but if I did have to go back to the *Norland*, at least, I thought, I'm going back to my sea family and the good times we always seem to have no matter what the circumstances.

But then to come back and hear about worrad happened to him. It was such a blot on the landscape. It suddenly made the *Norland* seem not quite the safe haven we always thought it was, especially as our job was still ferrying unfamiliar troops as well as supplies about. So when the news came shortly after arriving back that the MOD was finally releasing the *Norland* from military service and she could go back to civilian life, we was all made up.

JOHN

I had bought a video camera over the Christmas break with some of the bonus money I'd earned from being down in the Falklands. Sony it was, really big and heavy too, more like something from a TV studio, not like what you can get these days. Anyway, when I got back I started filming everything, especially on the day of our final departure, 6 January 1983. It was quite a sight as we was escorted out to the open sea by most of the support ships and navy ships still stationed around the islands. The *Yorkshireman* tug, our fellow ship from Hull, drew alongside us with the Queen's Own Highlanders' brass band gathered at the bow playing *Sailing* by Rod Stewart. That's a sentimental piece of music at the best of times, but if you thought about the lyrics as the band played the tune that day it really sent a frigging lump up in your throat, I tell you. All the crew on board the *Yorkshireman* was waving us off, probably wishing they was going back with us to Humberside, while another tug started to shoot jets of water from her firefighting gear in a display of honour towards the *Norland*. Every ship in the vicinity was sounding its foghorn, amazing to hear.

My mate Chuddy (Alan Eastwood who was a steward on the

ship) was standing beside me giving a little commentary over all this as I filmed it and at one point I can hear him saying, 'This is truly marvellous, but of course this is only a small send-off compared to what must be waiting for us back in Hull.'

WENDY

Little did we bleeding know!

JOHN

So Chuddy's commentary goes on as I focus on the band:

'They've been playing for us for nearly an hour now. Getting closer and closer to the ship so we can appreciate the music. It's bloody great. Never expected anything like this. It really is marvellous and shows just how much we've been appreciated down here.'

But the words we was about to hear was even more like music to my ears than what the brass band played that day.

General Thorne, commander of the British Forces in the Falklands, boarded *Norland* and we all gathered together in the for'ard lounge, just as we had gathered all them months ago, waiting to hear what Captain Ellerby was going to say, the day he told us our little passenger ferry was about to go to war, the day that changed our lives for ever. This time General Thorne stood up in front of us all and spoke these words:

'I feel a particular affinity for the crew of the *Norland*, believe it or not. Why? Well because you have looked after and cared for 2 Para, and now 3 Para also, just as I have looked after and cared for them. Of course they have cared for us too, fought and done great things for us. Total team effort we're involved in here, see? And that's why I can say with complete conviction that we have four great pillars supporting our country. The Navy, the Army, the Air Force and you, the merchant marines.'

A big cheer went up when he said that. It really meant a lot to us to hear that from him, dint it? He also said:

'You will not be forgotten. And should there be another crisis I know I'd want the *Norland* to serve with us again because the kind of service we'd receive would be unique. Caring, good-humoured and steadfast. I salute you all.'

And he did salute us as he left and we cheered and clapped as if we was at a football match or summat.

KEITH

So it was pretty much just us crew rattling round the *Norland* as she headed for Ascension for the final time. John went around filming all over the ship and it looked eerie with all those big spaces like the restaurant, which had been full twice over every mealtime for months now, sitting completely empty. We hardly knew what to do with ourselves, but never had there been such a sense of relief. The air warmed up around as we approached the tropics, and you could stand out on deck and literally feel the breeze blowing all the tension away, which you hardly knew had been there all these months, you'd got so used to it, like.

The only other non-crew members was two of the Royal Corps of Signals, who had to stay on board with all the hi-tech communications equipment that had been installed before we'd left Portsmouth. All the encryption and coding devices that received top secret messages from all over the place had to be looked after and then securely dismantled when we got back to England.

So I s'pose we still could have been a target for someone out there in the South Atlantic with no one to escort us all that way home.

SHEP

Except there *was* someone escorting us. We just never knew it. Until a few days out, when I was on the starboard side checking up on the lifeboats and suddenly the water bubbles and then roars and this bloody great submarine emerges from the waves alongside us. I nearly fell over the side, it was such a shock. Especially when this officer poked his head out the conning tower and salutes us, before he disappears along with the submarine beneath the waves again. It seems they was there all the time looking after us, but like the sub on the way to Montevideo, they wasn't allowed to reveal themselves, until it was all over.

JOHN

Once we got to Ascension we was split into two groups again, which was frigging annoying. Half of them (Frankie, me, Jeanie included) stayed on the ship to sail it back up to Hull and the other half of us (Keith, Dave, Shep, Wendy and them) was put on a plane and flown straight home to RAF Brize Norton.

WENDY

Then from Brize Norton back to Humberside airport. It wasn't quite the big homecoming into King George Dock we had imagined, but we was told when the *Norland* reached the Humber a week or so later we would be taken out to meet her at Immingham so we could all come in together for the final hurrah, you know't I mean?

Although as we landed in Humberside there was something going on which I couldn't quite make out at first. There was something on the tarmac ahead of the plane. It was some*one*, flapping about in a gigantic Union Jack costume. And as we got closer, and the plane nearly ran her over, I realised it was Candy. Worra sight she was! But it was nice to have such a welcome. She'll tell you she was dancing about in a giant caftan, but I think it was more like an old double duvet cover, God love her!

We had barely been back a day when me and Candy got straight back on the circuit together doing our drag act. But this time we did loads of shows for charities like the South Atlantic Fund, which was the first charity set up to help veterans of the Falklands conflict.

And as for the piano what we borrowed from Reverend Andrews at the port mission, the one what I promised him we'd bring back in one piece coz we was only popping down to Ascension then we'd be right back, not going anywhere near the Argies, you know't I mean? Well, that piano, being shoved all over the ferry, from one bar to the next, played every night amid the beer and the brawls, well it had seen as much action as we had, ant it? And in the end it collapsed under the strain.

FRANKIE
Oo, sounds like she's talking about me, dunt it?

WENDY
Luckily this family in Beverley, when they heard our story, donated a piano to the Flying Angel Seamen's Mission, so the Reverend, he

was very happy with that. And we couldn't be wirrout one, could we now, so we did a whip round and we raised three hundred and twelve quid to buy a new piano for the ship.

12

THE GRAND
FINALE?

KEITH

So some of us was home and we was made up about that. But we was ten days or so ahead of the *Norland*. And that didn't feel right. She was still on her way back up north from Ascension.

BOB

She eventually arrived off the east coast of England on Sunday 30 January as planned.

The official homecoming celebrations had been scheduled for the morning of 1 February so *Norland* was in fact two days early, captained now by Derek Wharton, my relief. His orders then were to anchor in the Humber estuary after spending the day meandering across Bridlington Bay, which created quite a sensation for the local residents, this war-torn, rust-streaked hulk of a ship coming through the winter mists. The plan was that our sister ship *Norstar*, together with a flotilla of smaller vessels, would rendezvous with *Norland* in the estuary and escort her to her home port, King George Dock. And arrangements had also been made for we crew members who had already arrived home to be picked up by *Norland* at Immingham coal terminal for the grand finale, as it were.

That night of 31 January storms whipped up along the Humber. Gale force winds turned to hurricane force at times and conditions in the Humber were some of the worst recorded in many years. Conditions were so extreme in fact that *Norstar* was unable to meet up with *Norland* and there was some question whether the *Norland* could even get into Immingham, what with a rapidly ebbing tide and ninety-mile-an-hour winds.

Meanwhile, back in Hull, we were all up at 3am getting into our best bib and tucker and I, bleary-eyed, went to pick up chief engineer Lloyd from his house. It was 4am when I reached his place and I'm banging on the door and no one's answering. After a good quarter of an hour or so I was ready to kick the door down, because I knew he wouldn't miss this for anything, like the rest of us. Anyway, I supposed I was more bleary-eyed than I thought as I eventually realised I was hammering on the door of the wrong house. Perhaps I should have realised from that ominous beginning that this day was about to go from bad to worse.

We all rendezvoused, some of us a little later than the rest, at King George Dock. All were counted present and correct, Don Ellerby included, then we bundled onto a bus which had been hired to take us to Immingham.

KEITH

We made it to Immingham, to the coal terminal where we was meant to meet up with the *Norland*. We all of us clambered off the bus, keen to see our beloved ship again. But she was nowhere to be seen.

BOB

Derek Wharton had been having a hell of time negotiating the bad weather, so much so that he could not dock at Immingham and had to sail back downriver to wait at Spurn Point for things to improve.

'You'd better hurry up, Derek,' I thought, 'Otherwise there's going to be a mutiny!'

How bloody ironic! We had steered the *Norland* through some of the most treacherous waters on the planet, freezing volatile conditions with icebergs at every turn, we had survived air raids, travelled under threat for thousands of miles and now she couldn't even get down the bloody Humber estuary! I should have read the signs when I was stood outside God knows who's door at four o'clock that morning.

KEITH

So we was all stood on the coal jetty in gale force winds waiting and waiting, gerrin more and more pissed off until we was given word that our *Norland* would not be making it in anytime soon. There was nothing for it but to hightail it back to King George Dock for the reception. We might as well not miss the party as well as the ship. So we clambered back onto the bus and it was only then that we looked down at our lovely pristine white shirts and saw they was covered in soot what the wind had been whipping about the coal terminal. And our faces, well, some of us looked like the black and white minstrels.

WENDY

I prefer to think of my look as more Dusty Springfield. Not for the first time, you know't I mean?

BOB

So in true *Carry On* style we all bundled back onto the bus out of the hurricane force winds, looking filthy and raced out to the Humber Bridge to cross over the estuary to Hull itself. The Humber Bridge had only been open since 1981 at which point it was the longest single span suspension bridge in the entire world and, lo and behold, there was a road block at the entrance with a big sign saying: BRIDGE CLOSED DUE TO HIGH WINDS.

Although Don was on board I was kind of the senior officer on the bus so I took it upon myself to instruct the driver to ignore the signs and the police and drive on over the bridge. Well, we had been in the midst of a battle zone, locked horns with the Royal Navy, fought for Queen and country; feeling suitably military by this time, we weren't going to let a little thing like the police and a roadblock stop us from getting to our party. It reminded me of chasing that RFA supply ship round the Falklands. The lengths I go to for a bloody beer!

The driver did as I asked, leaving the police in their cars looking on agog, but once we got right onto the bridge I realised the sense in having the roadblock. The wind was so strong that the bus took on a severe list portside.

'Everybody to the starboard side!' I yelled.

And I had to yell because the air pressure was such from all that wind that the sky lights popped open, and so there was everyone out of their seats, cramming themselves, in their sooty uniforms, on the high side, getting pelted with rain and wind blowing in through the roof. It was a wonder the bus didn't topple over and end up at the bottom of the estuary.

Eventually we made it, somehow alive, to King George Dock, looking a right state. There were still lots of people there, but they were all taking shelter in the terminal building, because there was still no sign of the ship. And so we had the party without her. We held on as long as we could, but the civic dignitaries, government officials and high ranking officers from the forces were all getting fidgety and had to be other places and what not. The streamers and the balloons and the flags were sort of redundant and it all fell a little flat. We'd been up since three in the morning, we got to the dock around ten.

JOHN

We'd painted these banners and hung 'em over the side of the ship so everyone onshore could read 'em as we came in:

**NO ONE RAN AS LONG AS THE *NORLAND* DID
HULL BACK TO HULL 66325 MILES 287 DAYS**

It was as if those words was coming back to bite us now. As if we was going to have to run even longer and even more miles and days before we could finally get back home.

At least, members of 2 Para had jumped on board, which meant the world to us. They had actually joined us in Tenerife, but we wasn't allowed to berth in the port there, the Spanish government was not happy with the Brits I s'pose after the war with Argentina, so the lads had to be transferred via the smaller boats.

Anyway it was good to see 'em. After the war was over and they had all gone back to their families, they hadn't forgotten about us. Far from it. Turns out they couldn't wait to join us for the *Norland*'s homecoming. It was as important to them as it was to us.

FRANKIE

2 Para band was all stood on the for'ard deck, all in their ceremonial uniforms, rubbing their hands together furiously, trying to keep warm so they could actually play their instruments as the *Norland* began to dock in Hull. It was gerrin dark and as cold as the bloody Falklands, but the boys started knocking out military style tunes and them two drummer boys started twirling their feather dusters about again, stood there in their leopard print dresses. 'Oo, aren't you boys camp?' I laughed at them as I stood there in me masculine officers' steward's uniform. They didn't mind. We all gave as good as we got. They was part of the family now. Always would be.

BOB

Eventually the winds finally downgraded themselves to 'mere' gale force and Derek managed to bring the *Norland* into the dock. It was now ten o'clock at night.

FRANKIE

Well, I hadn't seen such a dirty-looking bunch of reprobates as them lot from the bus, since chucking out time near Tramp's Alley in the sixties.

JOHN

As we drew closer to the dock we was all hanging over the railings trying to spot our loved ones and crew mates in the gloom. Some of them had painted welcome back signs on bed sheets, they was waving flags and really cheering us as best they could, although they were all so cold and miserable having had to wait all frigging day. It was hardly the massive spectacle Chuddy had said we was bound to have on the video commentary back when we was leaving the islands. The thousands that had turned out at King George Dock Terminal Building for the big reception had all buggered off home by now; the dignitaries, the government bods and officers from the armed forces. We'd worked our frigging arses off for months in the middle of air raids, then had to wait months more working down in the freezing South Atlantic before we could get back home, but they couldn't even be arsed to wait for a half a day to welcome us back.

KEITH

But at least our families was all still there. That was all that mattered really, wunt it.

WENDY

And our boys from 2 Para was with us, which said a lot, you know't I mean?

There's this moment on one of John's videos where about ten of the soldiers line up for a photo on deck, this is just as the ship is coming into King George Dock, and they all smile for the camera, all smart in their red berets and uniforms, most of them with their pencil moustaches, what was fashionable at the time. And this one in the front, as the photo is taken, just for a laff, like, kisses the para next to him on the cheek. They all have a good laff about it, but I reckon if he had done that a year before, the other one would have brayed his bloody head in, you know't I mean? I just think that moment on the video shows just how much they had learnt from being with us lot on board the *Norland*, about affection, about live and let live…

KEITH

…about how a bunch of blokes cast away far from home, can respond to each other with affection, rather than with brutality, gay or not.

13

I WOULD HAVE MUCH PREFERRED A NICE BROOCH

KEITH

Days after the anticlimax of the homecoming it was back to work for me at Immingham Graving Dock where over the next three months the *Norland* was completely gutted, all the military hardware removed and millions more pounds spent on a refurbishment. My job was to meet with all the hospitality mangers about the new cabins and restaurants they was going to put in. It was a far cry from negotiating the maze of shipping containers on the car deck from which we had to squeeze 571,482 meals over the nine-and-a-half months we was a troop ship in the South Atlantic. And on 20 April 1983, almost a year to the day that she was requisitioned by the MOD, she was back sailing the relatively tiny Hull-Rotterdam route. We was all back in our old familiar roles and jobs and sometimes I had to pinch myself to know that the last year hadn't been some kind of weird dream.

JOHN

Back at home we had seen footage of the other ships like the *Canberra* coming back to England with all the pomp and circumstance, the hero's welcome, the streamers, the flags, red, white and blue balloons, the water jets, a massive flotilla of boats escorting her, the music, the frigging clear skies. We saw the soldiers, the paras, the marines, the navy lads, the air force boys on the telly lined up and standing to attention on the lawn at Buckingham Palace having their medals personally pinned to their chests by Prince Philip and Prince Charles.

And then one day this little envelope landed on the doormat at the pub, The Yorkshireman, where I was still living with me mam and dad. I think we might have been setting up for opening time or summat coz I saw this envelope, it was addressed to me, and I picked it up and opened it to find a medal inside. A Falklands Campaign Medal. For me.

'Look, Fred, look!' mam goes, looking over my shoulder as I'm staring at this thing, 'He's gorra medal. He's gorra a medal for being in the war.'

After all the tears, all the times she had said she wasn't lerrin me go to the Falklands and now she was made up about it coz I got a medal!

And it was funny coz my dad, who had told her to let me go, who was fine about me going off to a war, well, he was not happy at all now.

'A medal through the fooking post?' he goes, 'Are they tekkin piss, or what!'

I WOULD HAVE MUCH PREFERRED A NICE BROOCH

KEITH

This letter arrived at North Sea Ferries head office from Buckingham Palace:

> I am delighted to hear that at long last *Norland* is back from the South Atlantic. Welcome back to your home port.
>
> I, together with everyone in this country, was deeply impressed by the performance of the Merchant Navy in the South Atlantic campaign. I hear nothing but the highest praise for the officers and crew of *Norland* and of the superb contribution you made month after month, often in dangerous, difficult and disagreeable circumstances. I send my warmest congratulations and best wishes to you all.
>
> Charles

JOHN

So deeply impressed that he sticks the medals in the frigging post!

KEITH

We all received our medals in the same way. Through the post. It was unceremonious to say the least. And it did feel a little disrespectful, especially after what General Thorne had so kindly said about us as we was about to sail for home.

BRIAN

It came in a few wee pieces and so we even had to fit the things together ourselves. It was a real DIY job, you know?

FRANKIE

I would have much preferred a nice brooch.

BOB

The other crew of the *Norland*, which wasn't involved in the fighting, but relieved us and brought the ship back to Hull, understandably, were not given South Atlantic Medals at all. So they used to rather mockingly call us lot Audie Murphys, after the American soldier turned film star, one of the most decorated soldiers of World War Two, who had a chest full of medals. That was a little ironic since some felt so aggrieved at the way the medals were delivered.

SHEP

Look, fifty thousand merchant seamen lost their lives supporting the armed forces in the two world wars alone. And worrabout all the wars before and since? The Merchant Navy has always been there, the fourth pillar, as the General rightly said. My father sailed in the Russian convoys, got torpedoed three times. 2 Para had made it very clear how much they valued the fact we put our heads over the parapet, as it were, first, before any other ship in the entire British Task Force.

I couldn't help but get annoyed when I heard this old bird crowing down the pub about how her son had been part of the crew on the *QE2* and how he'd *fought in the Falklands*.

'No he did not,' I told her and everyone else that was listening to her shite, 'The *QE2* only ever went as far as South Georgia, offloaded her troops and then turned around. I know, coz I was there.'

It wound me right up because I know what it felt like to be in San Carlos, being bombed and shot at. Risking your life every day. I'm not saying we was like the soldiers in the trenches on land, losing limbs and that, but we could have been. When I see

Simon Weston and the rest I think, there but by the grace of God go I.

KEITH

I felt the same as the rest of the lads to be honest, so when it came to a meeting of the Merchant Seamen's Association at some back room in a pub in the city I took the bull by the horns, stood up in front of them all and suggested that it might be nice if the Merchant Navy was included in the memorials to the armed forces who fought in the Falklands what was due to be placed in Holy Trinity Church in the centre of Hull. The secretaries politely told me that that was never going to happen, so undeterred, like, I suggested a separate memorial for the merchant seamen, perhaps placed alongside the one for the Falklands forces what was being planned for the church.

SHEP

Some arsehole at the back shouted out, 'If we do that we might as well have one for the Girl Guides too.'

I nearly smashed their fooking head in, whoever it was.

KEITH

And they politely told me again that there just wasn't any money for that kind of thing.

JOHN

Wasn't any money! Well, someone had some frigging money, I can tell you. North Sea Ferries, what owned *Norland*, had made millions from the MOD for having *Norland* down in the Falklands, but they never spent a frigging penny of it on commemorating the crew that went down there, that's for frigging sure. North Sea Ferries are a frigging disgrace and I don't mind who frigging knows it.

14

THE
LOVE BOAT

BOB

Two years after the Falklands, back on our usual run, I'm on the stern of the *Norland* in Rotterdam as we're loading the passengers in their cars, one of which stops by me and winds down its window. It's Tony Staples, the Wing Commander of RAF 18 Squadron, the guy that got me in trouble for taking that bloody Mercedes jeep off the Falklands. But a lot of water had passed under the bridge since then and I was genuinely happy to see him.

'Nice to see you, Bob,' he says, 'Will you meet me for a drink later?'

'Of course,' I said.

So once we had got away from Rotterdam I found Tony and we had a beer and chatted about old times.

'By the way, Tony, whatever happened to that G-Wagen we tried to bring back for you?'

'Oh, don't talk about that!' he says.

'Why not?'

'Well, we managed to get it back to Southampton and to our base, got it serviced and fired up, then applied to the MOD to see if we could get it plated so we could use it on the road as a squadron vehicle. And they said no, because "you weren't supposed to remove that jeep from the Falklands. In fact you need to surrender it to us and it will be confiscated." Well, stuff the MOD, I thought! We were on our way to Germany at the time, we'd just been tasked to go to Gütersloh for two years so we threw the jeep in the back of our Chinook and took it with us. Once in Germany, in order to get it on the road there, we wrote to Mercedes-Benz telling them we've lost the vehicle's documentation and can you give us some duplicates so we can get it registered. No problem, they say, just give us the identification number and the engine number and we will happily make the necessary arrangements.'

'Sounds good,' I said to Tony.

'Until a letter eventually comes back,' he says, 'from Mercedes-Benz saying, "Dear Wing Commander Staples, The G-Wagen in your possession has not been paid for."'

It seems Galtieri had ordered an awful lot of gear just before the war, but had never bothered to pay for any of it.

'So what did you do?' I asked Tony.

'We bunged it straight back in the Chinook and gave it to the MOD, just as they'd asked us to, of course!'

KEITH

Norland and her sister ship *Norstar* continued to be really very popular with the passenger trade. *Norland* could take up to twelve hundred passengers at a time, which is why the MOD thought she'd be good for taking all those troops south, and it was often full on those trips back and forth to the Continent.

BRIAN

The *Norland* was popular, I think, for crew and passengers, because it had those stabilizers and so didn't seem to be affected as much by rough weather, which let's face it is pretty common in the North Sea.

BOB

It was certainly one of the best ships I've ever sailed on, and I've sailed on a lot of ships over the years.

Talking of the stabilizers, it wasn't long after seeing Wing Commander Staples again, in June 1985, shortly after leaving Rotterdam, that the *Norland* sustained more damage than it ever had in the Falklands. Damage which by rights she shouldn't have survived.

Derek Wharton was captain that day, I was chief officer, on what turned out to be my last night ever as chief officer in fact. We were both on the bridge and suddenly Derek altered course to port. He had to take evasive action to avoid a collision with a German-registered coaster under the command of what turned out to be an allegedly drunken captain. Under full rudder the ship took on quite a list and I felt this jolt as her port side fin stabilizer touched the sea bed and was forced back up making a hole in the lower hull. Lights and alarm bells went off all over the place so I rushed to the panel and shut the watertight doors.

DAVE

Despite that, the main engine room flooded because for some reason the door was opened again after Bob had closed it from the bridge. One of the engineers down there noticed this and closed it again pretty quickly after, but by then there was debris in the seal around the door, so it continued to let in water and the main engine room was lost.

KEITH

I was on board that night. I went down for'ard with one of my colleagues, Ken, while another two went aft, to make sure there was no passengers left in the lower decks. And as me and Ken got down there I shined a torch up at this bulkhead to see what I thought was a massive crack. Well, suddenly there was an almighty noise and I thought this crack got even longer.

'Bloody hell, Ken,' I said, 'Did you hear that?'

There was no answer from Ken, so I looked round only to see him running for it. 'There's your answer,' I told myself, and legged it after him.

DAVE

In the aftermath you could see the tide mark at the top of the stairs that led from the engine room to G Deck. If the water had come that bit further over and into G Deck…well, people were living there, it doesn't bear thinking about.

KEITH

A Dutch tug rescued us that night and towed us back to shore. There was no casualties. Everything was fine in the end. It was just that the *Norland* was in dry dock for repairs for three months.

It was funny really that in all that time down in the war getting bombed and what-not we never had anything like that night in Rotterdam. And it was just as well coz it just shows you how bad it could have been if we did.

BOB

Derek Wharton was really shaken up by the events of that night in Rotterdam. He was a different person after that, in my opinion. Perhaps it didn't affect me in the same way, partly because I wasn't in command that night so didn't have the same responsibilities, but also probably because of what we had been through in the Falklands.

We had a pretty torrid time of it being bombed in San Carlos Water, but, having said that, we never saw the same horrors the soldiers did on land. So I can't say I was emotionally damaged by the experience of the war, but I do think most of us came back with a very different outlook on life. I certainly did.

DAVE

I wasn't as easy-going as I used to be after the war. By that I mean more forceful about what I wanted in life. I wrapped up my divorce pretty quickly and had no patience for bullshit anymore. Life's too short. You hear that often enough, but you really know it when you've been yards from a barrage of exploding thousand-pound bombs.

But it didn't have such a negative effect on many of us mainly, I believe, because we had taken our office with us, so to speak, down to the South Atlantic. Although what was going on outside was often bizarre and scary, once you went below deck things would look just like they always did if we were running from

Hull to Rotterdam and back, just like another day at work. Things were so familiar, because it was the ship we had all worked on for a number of years, it helped us feel more confident, I suppose.

WENDY

Well, I certainly did have some side effects from the war. After we got back I was living in a lovely brand-new flat by the river. I could see the ships coming and going up the estuary and everything. But worrit was, when the fog used to come down they would sound this foghorn, of course. But it sounded just like that bleeding klaxon we had down in the Falklands, dint it. And if it sounded when I was asleep it would make me sleepwalk. I s'pose I was running for cover in my sleep, you know't I mean? And I used to wake up in the living room, under the coffee table or with all me best crockery and the candelabra on top of me. Or I used to wake up in my bed having a panic attack and I couldn't see nowt, I was blind! For a couple of minutes until the shock wore off, then I got my sight back again, you know't I mean?

BRIAN

We were all in it together down there. Most of us had sailed together for years. We got on so well, on the whole, it made it easier to be so far away from home. It *was* our home. Home from home. I was at sea in total for thirty-nine years on many different ships and in all that time I had only two favourites: one of them was the *Norland*. There was something special about it.

WENDY

I think the angels thought so too, coz they was definitely with us down there in the Falklands.

BOB

It was a real community in all the best senses of the word.

BRIAN

Maybe, though, it was a good *time* to be on the *Norland* too.

DAVE

I think you've hit the nail right on the head there, Brian.

BRIAN

And if you put the same ship under today's working conditions I'm pretty sure you wouldn't enjoy it so much. It is pretty well documented, I think you'll find, that the golden era of the British Merchant Navy was the '60s and '70s. And we just won the lottery by being around and in it at that time.

BOB

Especially in the ferry industry. It was a very big growth industry in the '60s and '70s and we were fortunate enough to come into that branch of the Merchant Navy at a time when the company, North Sea Ferries, had taken the plunge on building the *Norland* and the *Norstar* which were the biggest roll-on/roll-off ferries in the world at that point. In the early sixties, families were not only beginning to be able to own a car, but also there was a growing trend for holidays abroad. Put these two things together and roll-on/roll-off ferries suddenly became very popular indeed. Not just as a means of getting to a destination, but as part of the holiday experience itself. And if it wasn't holiday makers in the summer season it would be the incessant freight that needed shifting all year round.

WENDY

Well, you had your bars and your discos and your swimming pools and shops, and we tried to make it like summat luxurious for the tourists: nice panelling, large ornate doors, flowers and silver cutlery on the tables and stewards smartly turned out... well, most of us anyway. It was the era of *Fantasy Island* and *The Love Boat*.

FRANKIE

Well, there was certainly plenty of love to be had on our boat, if you get me.

DAVE

You can get sentimental about a ship, as we all do about the *Norland*, but if you really look at it I think you'll see it's the people that make the ship. And that's what happened on the *Norland* in the seventies. We were already very close-knit before the Falklands. And if the Falklands never had happened we would still be as close. It's *because* we were that close already that the *Norland* was such a success during the war, I think.

WENDY

I got all sorts of offers when I was on the *Norland*.

FRANKIE

I bet you did!

WENDY

No, you daft cow! I was going to say, I got all sorts of offers from people in the entertainment industry, you know't I mean, when they saw me playing the piano and performing and that, especially after the Falklands. And I often wonder how far I could've taken it if I'd have said yes, if I'd put me mind to it. But, worrit was, I just couldn't leave the ship, could I? She was my ship. We was a family. And we was all about the families of the crew un'all. On the holidays when we was docked in Hull, sometimes we never went ashore, burr instead our families would all come on board. We'd purr a roast on for 'em, a carvery, the bar was open, there was me on the Joanna. We'd trim it up for Christmas, trim it up for Easter. Weddings, christenings, funerals, worrever, we was all there for each other, you know't I mean?

KEITH

In the mid-eighties, 1987 I think, the *Norland* and her sister ship *Norstar* was taken out of action for seven weeks while they went into Bremerhaven in Germany, where they was originally built thirteen years before, to be lengthened. She was literally sliced vertically down the middle into two halves, separated while a new twenty-metre section was floated in between and then the three segments was welded together to create a new jumbo ferry. It was quite an incredible sight. She was now a hundred and seventy three metres long and had thirty per cent more cargo capacity. It was also time for another refurbishment. All the cabins in G deck, where the crew lived and worked was taken out and made into space for freight. But because there was this new space on B, C and D decks they put more cabins there. Unfortunately the snug bar, what had been the officers' mess during the conflict and what had been renamed the Antelope Bar after, in honour of the warship and the crew that came on board us when she was sunk, was converted to more cabins.

WENDY

In March of that year, 1987, there had been the Zeebrugge disaster. The *Herald of Free Enterprise* was a ferry just like *Norland* and they let her go from the Belgian port of Zeebrugge one night with her bloody bow doors open. So the water flooded in and she capsized minutes after leaving the port, silly bastards. One hundred and ninety-three passengers and crew lost their lives that night. Can you imagine?

BRIAN

All because some eejit left the car deck doors open. That was when the ferries went dry for officers and crew. They stopped us all drinking throughout our days on board, which was probably good for safety...

DAVE

Although we managed to negotiate an entire war without any mishaps, certainly not on the Zeebrugge scale, whilst being allowed to drink. Come to think of it, it was sometimes the booze that kept us from going mad down there!

BRIAN

Things generally got stricter after Zeebrugge. More officious and so a lot less family-like. And the ferry companies, always looking for ways to cut costs, didn't help either. They gradually ran down the British crews and replaced them with Filipinos and Portuguese mainly because they were cheaper. In 1996 North Sea Ferries was taken over by P&O and in 2002 they sold the *Norland* to SNAV for use in the Mediterranean.

JOHN

There was a big do on board for her final voyage on the North Sea. Wendy played piano, we all turned out. The lads from 2 Para was there; they never missed anything to do with the *Norland*, all the reunions and that. Bob, coz he was UK director of North Sea Ferries by then, did a nice speech and then Royal Navy Commodore Mike Clapp spoke on behalf of the armed forces associated with the *Norland*.

COMMODORE MIKE CLAPP

The *Norland* to me is arguably the most remarkable ship that went south. To many of us she became a great friend, but she also earned an enormous respect and it's never easy to say goodbye to a friend. You might have thought that there had been worries from our end that a merchant ship was put into this position, a position where we would be under fire. I have to say that not one of the naval officers that were attached to the ships came to me and made any real complaint. Yes, they said they were worried, that was quite understandable, but the Merchant Navy proved themselves as steady as they had been before. And the fact that only six Merchant Navy men were killed out of some one hundred and seventy-four that died at sea is quite irrelevant because they were as much in the front line as any of us. I'm enormously glad it worked out that way but it was luck, nothing else. They were more at risk than the rest of us partly because of their gaudy painting, which showed them up for miles away and partly of course because they were largely totally unarmed.

KEITH

Even Rex Hunt, the Governor of the Falklands, came to say his bit about how much he respected the *Norland*, saying there was just two ships that hold special places in the hearts of the Falkland Islanders: one is HMS *Endurance* and the other is *Norland*.

JOHN

But that didn't stop 'em breaking her up in 2010, did it! She was the pride of Hull was that ship and it is so sad that she was scrapped and thrown away like a useless bit of metal. She was never that and the powers-that-be should hang their heads in shame that they let go a unique piece of history. It would have served this city well as a floating museum or hotel for all to enjoy for years to come. What is more unbelievable was that the council was trying to buy a frigging aircraft carrier to use as God knows what, which has no connection to Hull at all.

FRANKIE

But at least she had Keith tirelessly working to keep her memory alive, dint she? Tirelessly working to keep the memories of all the merchant ships and crews what went down to the Falklands in '82. Forget those fooking South Atlantic medals, Keith should be on the New Year's Honours list for what he's done since then, shouldn't he? Oo, I can see it now: Dame Keith Thompson!

15

GATHERING DUST AND RISING TENSIONS

2010

So it turns out Charles and Diana weren't so happily married after all. She died back in 1997 fleeing the paparazzi and he's now married to the woman Diana famously described as the third person in their marriage, Camilla Parker Bowles. The only vow Charles and Di managed to keep to each other, it seems, was not to name their son Stanley. They named him William and in the summer of 2010 the twenty-eight-year-old prince, serving in the RAF, was announcing his engagement to Kate Middleton.

Test tube babies were so passé. Now it was not a question of whether you could have a baby on IVF, but controversially what characteristics you wanted to choose for that baby by switching on or off various genetic codes in its embryonic DNA. If you were learning about this incredible news at home you could watch it on literally thousands of channels, hundreds of them devoted to news alone. Or you could watch on your laptop, of course, or even your phone. But if you'd rather play *Grand Theft Auto* or *Deathspank* then all you had to do was turn on your Playstation, Playstation 2, PS3, PSN, PSP, Wii, Xbox, Xbox 360, or Nintendo DS.

Cinema had survived the advent of the video recorder back in 1982 and now adults and children alike were flocking to see the seventh instalment in the *Harry Potter* film series or the third *Twilight* movie. Parents were less in tune with their children, however, when it came to them being excited by the news of some singer called Robbie Williams rejoining some band called Take That. For the kids it's all about JLS or Cheryl Cole, Lady Gaga, Tinie Tempah, Labrinth, Flo Rida and an array of other apparently lexically challenged individuals, whose reign at number one was more brief even than a political party leader's after losing an election. Fashion was moving faster than a finger over an iPad, the latest gadget to be released by Apple in the April of that year.

Also in April 2010 history was made with the first ever televised debate between the leaders of the three main political parties: Prime Minister Gordon Brown, David Cameron and Nick Clegg; and made again in early May with the first coalition government in British history to eventuate directly from an election.

What with all that excitement, not to mention Spain wining the World Cup in South Africa, Icelandic volcanoes spewing out enough ash to ground every plane in Europe for nearly a week, earthquakes devastating Haiti and killing 230,000 people, volcanic eruptions in the Pacific and an Ethiopian airliner crashing into the Mediterranean killing all ninety people on board, perhaps the resurfacing tensions concerning those little barren rocks in the South Atlantic known as the Falkland Islands to some, Las Islas Malvinas to others, slipped under the radar somewhat. But not to those who had lost loved ones or nearly lost their own lives serving as part of those four pillars General Thorne spoke so highly of: the army, the navy, the air force and, of course, the merchant marine.

Keith, Bob, Brian, Shep, Frankie, John, Mally, Dave and Wendy all kept a keen eye on events from the comfort of their homes in and around Hull.

London and Buenos Aires had restored diplomatic relations back in 1990, but the status of the Falklands remained a sore point, with disagreements over flights to the islands and fishing rights. The dispute had again come to the fore in 2009. In May of that year, Britain rejected a request by Argentina for talks on the future sovereignty over the islands. In December, the Argentine parliament passed a law laying claim to the Falklands, along with nearby South Georgia and the Sandwich Islands, in a move rejected by the UK.

In February 2010, the lads watched tensions rise further when a British company began searching for oil near the Falklands. Earlier in the month, Argentina had responded to the drilling plans by introducing new rules requiring all ships travelling to the Falklands through its waters to have a permit.

Perhaps this was one of the straws that broke the camel's back as far as Keith was concerned. As Frankie mentioned, he had been campaigning tirelessly since the Merchant Seamen's Association poured cold water on his dream of a memorial to the merchant seamen and women who served in the South Atlantic, which could stand proudly alongside those of the armed forces in Holy Trinity Church, Hull. Undeterred, he had kept their memory alive by organising annual remembrance services and parades, but the tipping point was when he heard that his beloved *Norland* had been taken to a giant scrapyard in India to be broken up for ever. All that remained of the ship was her bell and her battle honours. And Keith was determined not to let these last vestiges of her epic story end up gathering dust in a store cupboard somewhere in the P&O offices in London, which is exactly what the battle honours were doing. The missing bell was eventually spotted by Pete McWatt, who had been one of the cooks on the *Norland* during the Falklands alongside Mally. It was on display, some might say a little incongruously, in the VIP lounge of the P&O Dover to Calais ferry MS *Spirit of Britain*. Knowing how passionately Keith felt about it, Pete contacted him and so the campaigning resumed.

After extensive talks, Holy Trinity had declared that they were happy for Keith to organise a memorial and to place it in the church, so Keith met with P&O managers and explained to them that he wanted the bell to be the centre point of such a memorial, should anyone ever be able to raise the money to pay for it. Whilst Brian Rees, head of press and public relations, proved a great asset to Keith during his campaigning, P&O were keen to point out that the bell was worth £22,000 and the battle honours £15,000. Holy Trinity were kind enough to include them both on their archives insurance but only if they were encased for their own protection. So Keith called on everyone he could think of for assistance and eventually a local glazing firm said they would create the case for him at a discounted rate, since it was for such a noble cause. The glass case in which the bell would be placed would be framed with solid steel and would cost around £500 alone, even after the discount. Perhaps P&O (or North Sea Ferries as they were known back in 1982, when they were compensated copiously by the government in return for the requisitioning of the *Norland* and reaped the rewards of all the publicity garnered from having a ship heroically return intact from serving in a war) would be keen to chip in a few pounds?

JOHN
Would they frigging 'eck as like!

A budget of around £3,500 was now looking necessary to complete the memorial Keith had envisaged. With the Merchant Navy Association and P&O seemingly tighter than a nun's fanny, as Frankie might say, Keith was at the end of his tether. Head in hands he thought about the ISA he'd paid into at his local building society a number of years back. Money put away for a rainy day, as anyone would. Money he could use to supplement his pension now in the ninth year of his retirement. Money he could spend on his daughters or grandchildren, on those landmark occasions that would punctuate their lives and are always notoriously pricey. He thought of the ISA because it had £3,500 in it. It was a no brainer, as far as Keith was concerned. Someone had to pay for it. And if nobody did there would be no memorial. And to someone like Keith, that just wasn't acceptable. It was unthinkable in fact. Anyone who's ever laid a wreath or worn a poppy, or even placed a flower on a loved one's grave should understand that. So he pulled on his jacket, combed the now white hair on either side of his smooth pate, the anxiety there kissed away by his wife Jayne and her unreserved support, and he trudged to the building society on the high street to withdraw all the money from his savings.

2011

As the thirtieth anniversary of the war approached, the Argentine government sought to increase pressure on Britain by persuading members of the South American trading bloc Mercosur to close their ports to ships flying the Falklands flag.

2012

In what it described as a 'routine' move, the British government dispatched one of its newest destroyers, HMS *Dauntless*, to the South Atlantic to patrol the Falklands coast. Buenos Aires responded by formally complaining to the UN that Britain was 'militarising' the area. The Falkland Islands government decided to counter Argentine claims by scheduling a referendum on the status of the islands, saying that it wanted to 'send a firm message to Argentina that the islanders want to remain British'.

2013

The islanders voted almost unanimously in favour of remaining a British overseas territory.

2014

Far from begrudging the spending of his savings, Keith is proud that the memorial is now complete and accessible to anyone who wants to take the time to remember the part played by the Merchant Navy in the Falklands conflict; those who lost their lives; those who survived. It took until 2014 for P&O to finally relinquish their grasp on the bell and battle honours, publicly declaring that they were generously *loaning* them to Holy Trinity Church for the memorial in a ceremony on board the *Pride of Hull* ferry on midsummer's day that year.

Bob Lough was asked to present the treasures to the Reverend Canon Dr Neal Barnes of Holy Trinity, though I'm sure Bob would be the first to say he wasn't giving them away that day or even loaning them; he and all his *Norland* officers and crew were gaining them back from an inappropriate fate gathering dust in a gloomy store room or as mere decoration on a cross-channel ferry.

The bell particularly is a physical symbol of the familial spirit that resonated through every cabin, lounge, mess, galley, alleyway, bulkhead and even the holes left in them by Pervy; around every deck and in the hearts of every officer and crew member who made the *Norland* the *Love Boat* of the North Sea; who made it a mobile home for affection even in the frigid, bleak and black waters of the South Atlantic, even with a load of trained killers on board. And it was the people, just as Dave Risby so lucidly told me, which made the ship what it was for that brief window in a history littered with devastation and conflict.

If it had been about the decks and the cabins, the lounges and the amenities, the engines and the forecastle, the rudder and the bridge, those nine hundred soldiers of the 2nd Battalion, the Parachute Regiment, more used to being airborne than on the high seas, having just fought some of the bloodiest, most traumatising, cruel battles of recent times, surely would have grabbed the first ride home, especially when that ride was a luxury cruise liner destined for a hero's welcome with all the trimmings in a Portsmouth teeming with loved ones and flag-waving members of a patriotic public. But no, these soldiers with their trench foot, battle wounds, grief and home-sickness waited a further five precious days, after the unscathed *Canberra* swanned back up north, for the *Norland* to return from Argentina; the war-torn ship with the rust and the basic rations, stained and whiffing no doubt of the unwashed, infected, broken victims of their victory, no matter how hard the stewards had worked to mop and scrub after the POW's repatriation; these blood-stained Brits, the incarnation of macho, waited patiently for the ship with the sea queens and the poofs and the piano to take them on the long journey home. Because it was there on that ship that they knew they would find the welcome they craved, the affection they yearned for and most importantly the arena in which it was safe to express that yearning. The presence of a huge percentage of those soldiers, now in their fifties and sixties, each year in Hull at one of those *Norland* reunions, having travelled from all corners of the country, attests to this.

The men of 2 Para share a bond with the men and three women of the *Norland* which is unbreakable; not to mention their incomparable ability to drink a place dry.

EPILOGUE

2015

A few days before I first set eyes on Wendy playing piano in a pink satin shirt on the BBC's *One Show* – before I knew anything about the story of the *Norland* and its complement of unsung heroes, a story which has been as eye-opening for me as I hope it has been for you – Britain's Defence Secretary Michael Fallon announced plans to increase security spending in the South Atlantic to counter Argentina's attempts to improve its military. Argentina still poses a 'very live threat' to the British-ruled Falkland Islands, he warned. He told Parliament that the government planned to spend 180 million pounds over the next ten years to boost the security of the islands as part of a defence review.

'The principal threat to the islands remains,' he told legislators. 'I am confident that, following this review, we have the right deployment.'

The minister's announcement came as Argentina was trying to upgrade its military capabilities. It had looked at buying new warplanes and had apparently signed a co-operation deal with Russia that could result in it leasing Russian bombers in return for beef exports.

So the threat of another Falklands War it seems is never far away; indeed has never been far away since Argentina gained its independence from Spain in the early nineteenth century. Should another war ensue, the Merchant Navy would no doubt be called upon in larger numbers than ever.

The gents from the *Norland* continue to watch the news anxiously.

If they were still young and serving on the ships would they go back now if their vessels were requisitioned?

BRIAN

If I had to make the decision again now, knowing what I know and what I put my family through, then no, I would not volunteer again. We have a strong family and came through it OK, quickly getting back to normal, but for a few there were big problems, divorces and such.

Brian's view is pretty much echoed by every one of the lads. And perhaps it would be by many of the soldiers that fought in '82, given the startling statistic that, during the ensuing twenty-five years, more Falklands veterans committed suicide than the two hundred and fifty-five that died during the hostilities.

In 2002 Denzil Connick, the co-founder of The South Atlantic Medal Association, blamed the suicide rate on the 'stiff upper lip brigade' and a lack of resources to tackle Post Traumatic Stress

Disorder (PTSD). The ex-paratrooper, who lost a leg in the Falklands, said: 'Nobody knows the official figures for suicides. That is one of the problems. But we know for sure we have lost an average of ten veterans per year since the conflict ended.' Mr Connick, himself a PTSD sufferer, added, 'Unfortunately, one of the things about PTSD is that you can get other conditions associated with it such as alcoholism and drug abuse. Sufferers almost always have difficulty forming relationships and some have flashbacks or difficulties in crowded areas such as supermarkets.'

The Ministry of Defence refused to comment on this subject until, in 2013, a study was published which claimed there is no difference in the suicide rate of Falklands veterans as compared to the general population. But it may not surprise you to know that this study was especially commissioned by the Ministry of Defence.

These are the debates around the statistics for the UK only, of course. But what about the figures for Argentinian soldiers? The suicide figures among them are even greater than the UK, it is reported. Those kids who were conscripted against their will, as unprepared and untrained as the crew of the *Norland*, but who had to endure unimaginable horrors, ill treatment and pain. No wonder they were so grateful and pleasantly surprised by the welcome they received from those tender-hearted, strong-willed British merchant seamen on board the M.V. *Norland*.

★　★　★

Roy 'Wendy' Gibson served on North Sea Ferries for twenty-seven years. After the Falklands he was promoted to Restaurant Manager by his new boss, the now Chief Purser, Keith. With their drag act, Wendy and Candy went on to raise thousands of pounds for various charities supporting service men and women. Wendy retired in 2001 and lives in Cottingham, near Hull, with his pussy.

Frankie Green served in the Merchant Navy for twenty years, then opened a pub in Hull, called the Vauxhall Tavern. He retired in 2000 and, not to be outdone by Wendy, he lives happily in Hull with his pussy too.

John Foster met Audrey when she came to work on the *Norland* as a croupier in 1983. They were married in 1984 and are still happily married today with two sons. In 1991 they left the Merchant Navy and started running a pub in Hull, called, of course, The *Norland*.

'Not a day goes by, that I don't think about the happy memories on board MV *Norland* and her sister MV *Norstar*. We miss you both, RIP.'

Jeanie Woodcock, having become increasingly infirm, spent her final years in Lake View Manor nursing home in Pearson Park.

Keith, Wendy, Frankie and others from the *Norland* would often go to the home in west Hull and take her out in her wheelchair.

'Now remember,' the nurse would say to the lads as they left, 'No alcohol for Jeanie. Not with the medication she's on.'

'Right you are,' they'd say, 'We're only going for a walk round the park or summat.'

And when they got clear of the home Jeanie would pipe up, 'We are not going round no bleeding park!'

'Course not,' the lads would say, 'We're going down the pub.'

And so an afternoon of drinking and reminiscing would ensue. Jeanie would be on the Bacardis, of course. No double-doubles. Just a small treble! And she would come alive again. Just as she used to be the life and soul of the ship. Such a powerful presence among all those blokes.

But then it was time to go back to the nursing home. Jeanie was a bit the worse for wear by this time, to say the least, so her friends would wheel her back to the front door, ring the bell and leg it before they got a telling-off by the nurses!

Jeanie passed away in 2008. She was seventy-seven, but she never faded away. She would have hated that. She refused to go and lie on her bunk when the air raids were raging in '82. She would rather be marching round the decks in her oversized tin helmet and her life jacket, waving her little Union Jack. And that was how she was when it came to life in general, throughout her earlier years, as well as in her twilight. She refused to take it lying down. So the lads would often whisk her away, out of God's waiting room, and back into life. Get her pissed, just as she wanted to, right up till closing time.

Keith Thompson retired in October 2001 and found it hard to relax, having been at sea since he was fifteen years old, first as a galley boy on a trawler. So he found himself helping the elderly on a local sheltered housing project while, as we have seen, keeping the memory alive of his fellow merchant marines. A yearly service is now held at Holy Trinity Church, where Keith volunteers, attended by numerous veterans, the collections at these services going to help both the church and veterans.

Aged sixty-seven, Keith, and others attending a men's health night at the church, were encouraged to ask their GPs for a routine check for prostate specific antigens in the blood. Keith went for his check and was told he had very high levels of PSA. A biopsy at a local oncology centre revealed he had an aggressive form of prostate cancer.

'It's the most horrible thing to be told you've got cancer. I wasn't listening. I was thinking about my will, my funeral and my family's future.'

A week later and Keith was having surgery to remove the cancer. Things are now looking up for Keith, but instead of counting his own lucky stars, in true Keith style, in true *Norland* '82 style, in fact, he went out to help others, campaigning to raise awareness in men of the need for routine testing to catch such diseases early enough to treat them.

Bob Lough, having been captain of both the *Norland* and *Norsea*, became UK Director of P&O North Sea Ferries in 1993 until 2003 when he took early retirement. However, never one to twiddle his thumbs, Bob soon found himself the International Safety Manager at Wilson Yacht Management 'looking after yachts for the squillionaires of this world'. At seventy years old, this grandfather of four should have retired, but just cannot seem to make the break with life at sea, although where he finds the time for marine work between rebuilding French houses, piloting gliders and restoring classic cars is beyond me.

Brian Lavender retired in October 2001 after seeing many changes in the shipping industry.

'The company still gives us free ferry travel with our cars and its very useful to us as our son lives and works in Amsterdam. However, when I travel I don't know anyone on the ships now.

Unlike some, I never returned to the Falklands and I have no real desire to, although I have been back to Vietnam since retirement with my family three times.'

Dave Risby left *Norland* in 1987 to sail on *Norsea*. However, after just a few years he rejoined the *Norland*. Despite stints on both *Norbay* from 1994 and *Pride of Hull* from 2001, he was there for the *Norland's* farewell voyage in February 2002 before retiring two months later.

Brian 'Shep' Shepherd became an active member of the Merchant Navy Association, Hull branch, after retiring, and is now a regular attendee at their services and parades.

Malcolm 'Mally' Gelder retired from North Sea Ferries in 2004 and spends many a happy day now with his family, wife Josie and dog Max.

ACKNOWLEDGEMENTS

Keith, my admiration for your quiet, but tenacious, dedication to a cause knows no bounds. Thanks for organising everything when it came to meetings with the lads. I am so glad I stumbled across you. I hope this book will go some way to helping keep the memories you treasure alive.

Wendy, thanks for the hospitality and the sandwiches for the train! You are a true carer and I understand now why 2 Para waited for you and the *Norland*.

Frankie, what a joy it has been getting to know you. Thanks for trusting me with your stories.

Candy, thanks for painting such a colourful picture of life on the *Norland* before the Falklands.

Wendy, Frankie and Candy, thanks for being the bastions of camp you are. For that alone, in a society which still fails epically when it comes to prejudice, you are heroes.

Mally, thanks for covering everything from egg and chips to emotional turmoil in the short time we spoke.

Dave, thanks for your humour and honesty from the start.

Shep, thanks for providing the drama. Tall tales or not, you tell them well.

Brian, thanks for all the photos, documents and responding to all my questions in such mind-blowing detail. You've really helped this layman get a better grip on the complex workings of a merchant ship.

Bob, thanks for the hospitality and access to your archive. I remember you saying on the phone that you couldn't believe anyone would be interested in the story of the *Norland*. Well, I can't believe anyone *wouldn't*. I hope I've done it, and your enormously significant and courageous part in it, justice.

John, thanks for the priceless videos and photos, and for being the last man standing in the bar of the Royal Station Hotel on our first meeting back in June 2014.

Lloyd Newell, thanks for taking time out from caring for your wife to furnish me with some valuable technical details and tales.

Thanks to my friends and family, as ever, for their enthusiasm and support during the writing of this book.

Thanks to Ian Golding: the dude, and my editorial guru.

Thanks to all at John Blake Publishing.

APPENDIX I

CREW LIST – MV *NORLAND* AS OF 11 MAY 1982

Donald Ellerby – Master (Captain)

Bob Lough – Chief Officer

Christopher Cammish – Second Officer

Richard Woof – Second Officer

David Risby – Second Officer

Lloyd Newwell – Chief Engineer

James Draper – Second Engineer

David Bales – Third Engineer

Francis Waller – Third Engineer

John Dent – Third Engineer

Dereck Begg – Third Engineer

Herbert Slater – Electrician

Brian Burton – Electrician

Derrick Frizzell – Third Engineer

Brian Lavender – Radio Officer

John Crowther – Purser

John Graham – Assistant Purser

Keith Thompson – Assistant Purser

Harold Sutherland – Shop Manager

John Laycock – Able Seaman

Michael Temple – Able Seaman

Raymond Scruton – Able Seaman

APPENDIX I

Robert Reeves – Petty Officer Motorman

John Whitelam – Petty Officer Motorman

Frank Altoft – Petty Officer Motorman

Brian Shepherd – Able Seaman

William Hookem – Chief Petty Officer

Michael Failey – Able Seaman

Thomas Clark – Able Seaman

Kenneth Slaughter – Petty Officer Motorman

Dereck Zeese – Carpenter

Patrick Dolan – Able Seaman

Raymond Shirtliff – Able Seaman

Raymond Dennison – Able Seaman

William Moody – Steward

Joseph Whelen – Steward

Barry Myers – Steward

Martin Evans – Steward

Frank Green – Steward

Andrew Robinson – Steward

James Foster – Steward

Stephen Butcher – Steward

Harold Dixon – Steward

Steven Isham – Steward

David Aistrop – Steward

Ronald Whincup – Steward

Richard Johnson – Steward

Douglas Gibson – Steward

Peter Smith – Steward

Jean Woodcock – Stewardess

Peter Samsan – Steward

Shirley Howlett – Stewardess

Alan Temperton – Cook

Timothy Hardisty – Cook

Terence Stephenson – Steward

Graham Edwards – Steward

Robert Gair – Steward

Reginald Kemp – Steward

Ernest Fuller – Steward

Leslie Marrow – Steward

Nigel Rounding – Steward

Michael Atkinson – Steward

Cyril Suter – Steward

Leslie Isham – Steward

Peter Knowles – Steward

Frank McNamee – Steward

Roy Gibson – Steward

Geoffrey Palframan – Steward

Donald Black – Steward

Christopher Sutcliffe – Leading Steward Storekeeper

Brian Wilson – Leading Steward

Christopher Foley – Cook

Leslie Carter – Steward

George Rimmer – Chief Cook

Stephen Chapman – Leading Steward Storekeeper

Peter 0'Mahomey – Steward

Malcolm Gelder – Cook

Anthony Palframan – Steward

Alan Eastwood – Steward

Malcolm Robinson – Steward

Kevin Hornsby – Steward

Michael Wingham – Steward

John Foster – Steward

Gary Holt – Steward

Karl Tungate – Cook

Kenneth Harry – Cook

Neil Woolin – Cook

Antony Wilson – Cook

John Lambert – Cook

Peter McWatt – Cook

Alan Richardson – First Radio Officer (RFA)

Reginald Collins – Shop

Roderick Hardwick-King – Shop

John Kenyon – Able Seaman

APPENDIX II

OFFICERS' DUTIES

Captain: no watch-keeping; in overall charge; visits bridge while entering and leaving port, last thing at night before turning in, in emergencies and in very bad weather. At other times, paper work and general admin.

Chief Officer: second in command, watch keeping 4am to 8am, 4pm to 8pm; in overall charge of cargo, loading and unloading ship, stability etc.

2nd Officer: watch keeping midnight to 4am, midday to 4pm; the navigator; in charge of plotting courses to various destinations; taking sun sights and star sights to determine ships position (before sat navs were invented); correcting charts etc.

3rd Officer (Junior Officer): watch keeping 8am to midday, 8pm to midnight; learning all of the above.

Chief Engineer: much like the captain, visits engine room while leaving and entering port, and during manoeuvres; in overall charge, but leaves running of engine room to the 2nd Engineer.

2nd Engineer: watch keeping 4am to 8am, 4pm to 8pm.

3rd Engineer: watch keeping midnight to 4am, midday to 4pm.

4th Engineer: watch keeping 8am to midday, 8pm to midnight.

Radio Officer: on watch 8am to 10am, midday to 2pm, 4pm to 6pm, 8pm to 10pm.

APPENDIX III

TECHNICAL DATA

Name: MV *Norland* (1974–2002)
  SNAV *Sicilia* (2002–10)
Owner: North Sea Ferries (1974–96)
  P&O North Sea Ferries (1996–2002)
  SNAV Aliscafo (2002–10)
Building yard: A.G. Weser, Bremerhaven, West Germany
Completed: June 1974
Port of Registry: Hull (1974–2004)
  Naples (2004–6)
  Funchal (2006–7)
  Naples (2007–10)
Services:
Hull/Rotterdam: June 1974–April 1982
  April 1983–May 1987
  (Requisitioned by MOD. April 1982–April 1983)

Hull/Zeebrugge: July 1987–February 2002
Naples/Palermo: March 2002–September 2010

BEFORE LENGTHENING

Gross tonnage (a ship's internal volume where 100 cubic feet =1 gross ton): 12,988

Deadweight tonnage (weight of cargo, stores, fresh water, passengers, crew, fuel and ballast a ship can carry when submerged to her loadline): 3,800

Displacement tonnage (total weight of a ship and her contents): 13,787

Length: 153m

Passengers: 1,243

Cargo: max. 500 cars or 134 x 12m units + 72 cars, or any mix

AFTER LENGTHENING (completed 28 June 1987)

Gross tonnage: 15,047 (or 26,919 after an international convention amendment of the calculation formula)

Deadweight tonnage: 5,000 approx.

Displacement tonnage: 17,000

Length: 173.25m

Passengers: 900

Cargo: max. 500 cars or 179 x 12m units + 72 cars, or any mix

Service speed: 18.5 knots (21 mph)

Draft (depth of water a vessel needs in order to float): 6.02m

FURTHER READING

I am indebted to the authors of a handful of fascinating works in helping me to complete this book.

For an insightful and detailed exploration of the world of camp and gay men on British merchant ships throughout the ages I recommend *Hello Sailor: the hidden history of gay life at sea* by Paul Baker and Jo Stanley. Published by Pearson (Longman), 2003.

For a meticulous look at the technical specifications of every merchant ship involved in the Falklands conflict please take a gander at *Merchant Ships at War: the Falklands Experience* by Captain Roger Villar. Published by Conway Maritime Press, 1984.

For a harrowing, first-hand account of what it was like for the soldiers of 2 Para during the Falklands conflict, read the disarmingly honest memoir *A Soldier's Song* by Ken Lukowiak. Published by Phoenix 1993.